D0019208

CAROLE P999
SESKO
5305877750

Coming soon!

*July & Winter: The Growing Seasons
of the Sierra for Farmers and Gardeners*

Find Gary and his farmers' market schedule
at www.sierravalleyfarms.com

Read Gary's column,
"Chronicles of a Dirt Farmer"
at www.moonshineink.com

Check out Gary and his farm on YouTube,
"Is Sustainable Attainable?"

WHY I FARM

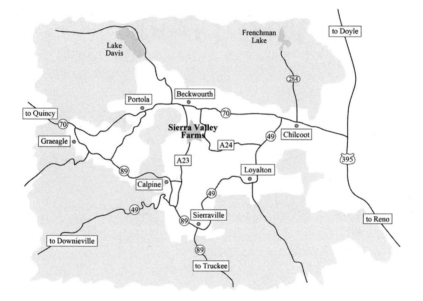

WHY I FARM
RISKING IT ALL FOR A LIFE ON THE LAND
Gary Romano

Bona Fide Books
Tahoe Paradise, CA

Copyright © 2013 by Bona Fide Books.

All rights reserved. No portion of this work may be reproduced or transmitted in any form or by any means, electronic or mechanical, including photocopying and recording, or by any information storage or retrieval system, without permission in writing from Bona Fide Books.

ISBN 978-1-936511-07-5

Library of Congress Control Number: 2013934320

Cover Design: www.shearermedia.com
Copy Editor: Mary Cook
Photo Imaging/Map Illustration: Jared Manninen
Layout: www.kristenschwartz.com
Printing and Binding: Thomson-Shore, Dexter, MI

Orders, inquiries, and correspondence should be addressed to:
        Bona Fide Books
        PO Box 550278, South Lake Tahoe, CA 96155
        (530) 573-1513
        www.bonafidebooks.com

In Memory

Of my mentor growing up,
my twin brother, Larry Romano.
Larry would get a few laughs out of this
as only he and I could relate to our
childhood experiences on the farm.

This book is dedicated to my family
and friends, and to all the small farmers
across America who do what they do.

If this book saves one small family farm
or inspires someone to become a farmer,
it will all be worth it.

The fight to save family farms isn't just about farmers. It's about making sure that there is a safe and healthy food supply for all of us. It's about jobs, from Main Street to Wall Street. It's about a better America.

~Willie Nelson

CONTENTS

INTRODUCTION

Farming looks mighty easy when your plow is
a pencil and you're a thousand miles from the
cornfield.

~Dwight David Eisenhower

If you look around, change is happening all over the world:
countries are overthrowing longtime governmental regimes,
dictators are being ousted, and in the United States, 2011 was
the "year of the protester," according to *Time* magazine, and
then came Occupy Wall Street. That's big time! Throughout
America and the world, the little guy is fed up with the systems
that govern us and that we've had to live by. Over the past few
years in the United States, we have seen demonstrations of the
99 Percent Main Street working class voicing their opposition
to the 1 Percent Wall Street, who are running this country. So I
thought, why not write about the 1 percent of the 99 percent,
the dinosaurs in today's workforce: America's small farmers.

Sixty years ago, small farms (those under two hundred
acres) accounted for more than 10 percent of American jobs;
today, we are losing hundreds of small farms every year—the
small farmer has dwindled down to a pitiful 1 percent of
today's occupations. In fact, small farmers are classified as
"other" according to the US census bureau. The slogan of the
twentieth-century farm was "get big or get out," dictated by
the industrial agriculture revolution after World War II. The
message to the small farmer was "join us or get out of the way
because here we come." And they did just that! In came the
transformers—like Dow Chemical, Monsanto, Cargill, and
General Mills—that created corporate factory farms filled with
monoculture and genetically modified organisms (GMOs), all
fed by petroleum-based products so that they could feed us
their Frankenfoods. These corporations infiltrated the United

States Department of Agriculture (USDA) and the U.S. Food and Drug Administration (FDA) to lobby legislators, set the subsidies, and develop rules and regulations in their favor, literally kicking the little guy out.

Their biggest victory wasn't just taking over the small farms, but also manipulating the American public by way of the media, labeling, and advertising. The corporations created a new way of advertising food products through public relations that had never been done before, all to coerce folks into buying food that wasn't healthy or sustainable. Over the years, the public relations departments of these large corporate food conglomerates have used marketing and graphics, advertising, and faulty labeling to con the general public into purchasing their products. Authors and public figures like Michael Pollan and Michael Moore are drawing attention to the fact that the foods we are now eating are not healthy, and are contributing to our obesity, cancer rates, and other medical disorders.

In the twenty-first century, we must reverse the damage that's been done to our food system, our land, and our occupations. We must go back to the earth, take back our farms, reeducate our children and the general public about where our food comes from, and create a positive environment to attract young and old people to farming again. But who am I to tell you what to do? I am just a small organic farmer operating in Sierra Valley, in the small town of Beckwourth, Plumas County, California. I'm not a famous author or celebrity, just one of the last 1 percent of today's occupations—I'm a farmer. This book is my story: my opinions, my humor and satire, the sweat and blood of three generations of farming in California. At fifty-five years old, I felt it was time to tell my story—a story from the trenches of someone who has seen successes and failures, and faces an uncertain future in trying to sustain a small family farm. I'm not a scholar or expert or published author in the subject of agriculture, but I'm a survivor, and I want to share my experiences and personal views as a small organic farmer with you.

My life as a third-generation farmer has been a metamorphosis: first, I was born into a strong Italian farming family and farmed throughout my childhood; then, like many youth, I resisted the only life I had known to get an education and went into a "cocoon," working in public service for my mid-years; next, I got a second chance to save the family farm and return to my roots; and finally, where I am now—trying to survive and find solutions to sustain the farm in the twenty-first century. The purpose of writing this book is to create food for thought and enlist farmers and consumers in a call to action. In this day and age, it is crucial to know where your food comes from and who is growing it. I want to put others in my shoes, to inspire new people to farm, and to give a chuckle to the old-timers who have gone through the same trenches as my family and me. I also want you to understand what real small farmers go through in trying to put that carrot on your plate. Not every chapter ends in a fairy tale, and there is some gloom and doom throughout the book, but real life doesn't always present us with a bed of roses. Farming is hard work, but life is good and can be better.

There are many challenges ahead for the small farmer to overcome, and many changes need to happen in the near future for small farms to survive. Media hype suggests that people are going back to farming, but the reality is that few survive in this day and age. This occupation represents the "survival of the fittest," and small farms must be more than fit to survive. As the owner of Sierra Valley Farms, a certified organic farm and native plant nursery located in the northeastern mountains of the Sierra Nevada range, I've written this book as a conversation with you. It's straight from the horse's mouth—there's no sugar coating on this baby! I want you to feel my emotions throughout the book, to agree or disagree—it's America! But most of all, I want you to think about your food and who is going to grow it in the twenty-first century.

To help you understand where I'm coming from, I begin by describing my family's farming history, and my memories of farming as a child, to get you in the frame of mind of what it was once like. As I went into my cocoon—working in public service for seventeen years—a lot of small family farms went under. But when I got another chance to return to farming, I jumped at it, realizing in retrospect that it wasn't so bad after all.

But times had changed.

The old ways of farming were long gone. Today, there is a lot more to farming than just growing a crop and going to market, like my dad and his father did. Now I have to be not only a farmer but also deal with advertising, marketing, and certifying myself as organic. I act as a distributor, an event coordinator, a media director, a writer, and even a "rock star" to bring attention to farming. And in spite of all of that, I still may not make it. I know us small farmers are a dying breed. In addition, I realize that my childhood was unique—not everyone comes from a farming background. Kids today have to look back to their grandparents or beyond for someone who was actually a farmer. There is a disconnect between kids today and farming— not knowing where their food is grown and who grows it. I'm hoping that my experiences, and maybe the solutions I set forth here, will trigger a local movement within communities to change the systems that strangle the small farmer. It's not an easy task; it's going to take policymakers, businesses, institutions, communities, consumers, and small farmers working together to change the current system and create a positive environment to attract, enhance, and protect the American small farm.

I had fun with this book. I hope you enjoy it, and I hope to write more. I'm not a professional writer, but in 1982 I self-published a trail guide on wild edible plants of San Luis Obispo County, California, and I also write a weekly editorial, "Chronicles of a Dirt Farmer," for *Moonshine Ink*, an independent monthly newspaper in Truckee, California. *Why I Farm: Risking It All for a Life on the Land* is my story. I've seen the struggles of my parents and grandparents up close, along with the trials and tribulations of my fellow farmers today. I feel I have some solutions to help sustain family farms and provide our own food sovereignty. Farming under the current rules and regulations of the USDA and state departments of food and agriculture is killing the small farmer. The odds are stacked against us, and in the long run it is a slow death—suicide with a butter knife, if you will—and if nothing else, it is a lifetime of frustration from trying to make a living. But it's the passion to farm that drives the farmer, not making it pencil out. It's a way of life: you live it, you breathe it, you live for it, *you are a farmer*. You can't learn it in school, and you can't teach it; you have to simply be it. There is no compromise! To all small farmers in America, I walk in your shoes and thank you for what you do. Let's stand together in this twenty-first century and go small, or not at all!

Giovanni and Bepino Romano, 1915

Chapter 1
LA FAMILIA

Opportunity is missed by most people because
it is dressed in overalls and looks like work.
~Thomas Edison

The Romano Flower Farm: Redwood City, California

The oldest son of a clocksmith in Campeggi, Italy, a small town located on the Mediterranean region of Genoa, Giovanni Lodovico Romano was recruited by his younger brother Bepino (Bep) in 1915 to come out to San Francisco and help start a flower business. Only seventeen years old, Giovanni set off to the land of opportunity, America. Bep, adventurous at the age of fourteen, left Italy to find some cousins who had come to San Francisco after the earthquake of 1906. He established himself in the North Beach area of San Francisco in an Italian neighborhood and found work in the local flower industry.

Once Giovanni arrived, the two brothers decided to try it on their own, but they were too much alike, *testa dura* (hardheaded) as Italians would say, so the brothers split up and started their own businesses. Bep opened the California Evergreen Nursery in Colma and later in Half Moon Bay with his younger brother Dario, who came out from Italy to become his partner in 1920. Meanwhile, Giovanni (Grandpa, or Nonno, as we would later call him) worked in the cut-flower business at the Fifth Street flower market in San Francisco for about five years and then decided to start a cut-flower operation, G. L. Romano Wholesale Florist, in Redwood City, California, in 1921. As most Italians did in those days, he wired back home for a wife, Nina, a girl he knew in his hometown. There is a running joke in the family that Grandma was a "mistake" because the wrong

Giovanni and Nina Romano, 1921

Nina was sent to Grandpa. It wasn't the girl he had asked for, but he married her anyway because he said she was prettier than the girl he originally requested. Her name was Nina Maria Scanavino, a beautiful woman, and they married in 1921. Notice Grandpa is sitting in the photo, because he was shorter than Nina. That's what they did in those days. (Heaven forbid a woman be taller than a man.) Soon after, Giovanni and Nina had two daughters, Inez and Mary, and in 1926 a son, Louis Romano, my dad. It was Nonno's dream to have a boy to help him in the flower business, and so it became G. L. Romano & Son Wholesale Florists.

Nonno bought three acres in Redwood City and began to farm gladiola bulbs, asters, cockscomb, and celosia as summer annual crops. He then planted perennial trees and shrubs for cut-flower production that he could depend on for income every season throughout the year. He grew early spring-flowering cherry, almond, and peach trees, and later added flowering quince and double-flowering lilacs. There wasn't much he could grow in late fall and winter, so he looked to see what Mother Nature had to offer out in the wild. Nonno traveled the mountains throughout California and Oregon, following the seasons. Fall was a time for foliage, and he cut boughs of maple, madrone, and oak as they turned color, selling them at the Fifth Street flower market in San Francisco. During the winter, his travels took him into the foothills and mountains of the Sierra Nevada for toyon and manzanita berries, mistletoe, and Christmas trees. He was best known at the flower market for his ability to climb huge sugar pines. With a single rope and a pole pruner, Nonno cut boughs of pine limbs with huge cones on them that he would sell for a high price to San Francisco wreathmakers. The five- to six-foot-long limbs cut from the ends of the sugar pine branches had anywhere from four to eight pinecones hanging from them, each up to eighteen inches long.

A master of seasons, Nonno knew what to cut in any month of the year and sell at the flower market. While he was out in

Mary, Louis, and Inez Romano, 1932

the countryside, Grandma (Nonna) was at home caring for the kids, milking the cows, making cheese and wine, and tending to the chickens. In 1933, Nonna died suddenly of a mastoid infection in her ear. My dad was only six years old, and he and his sisters carried on the farm with Nonno throughout high school, cutting flowers, doing the home chores, and working the flower market. Nonno never remarried; he raised the kids by himself, getting some help from his younger brother Dario's family.

Inez and Mary got married soon after high school and moved off the farm. Dad stayed on the property to help Nonno in the flower business. Nonno had survived World War I and the Depression, and his business started to grow by the 1940s. My dad was drafted into the Navy in 1945. He returned home after a short service and then was drafted again, this time into the Marines during the Korean War in 1952, but he spent most of his time at California's Camp Pendleton. Nonno had bought ten acres in Cupertino, California, in 1948 and began expanding the flower operation. When Dad returned from the Korean War, he settled down on the property in Redwood City.

Nonno and Louis Romano

The Bay Area was growing. There was a need for more schools, and in late 1956, Dad and Nonno got a letter from Santa Clara County that stated, by eminent domain, their land was going to be taken over for the Cupertino High School and they had to move. Eminent domain is the action of a state to seize a citizen's private property with due monetary compensation, but without the owner's consent, usually devoting the purchase for public use, in this case, a new school site. Santa Clara County paid a fair price, and Dad and Grandpa bought a twelve-acre ranch along Coyote Creek in San Jose, California.

The Folchi Ranch: Beckwourth, California

It all started with a dream, a dream Giacamo Folchi (Grandpa) had in 1907 when he left Ellis Island as an Italian emigrant. His dream was to be an American rancher. He wound up in Watsonville, California, then Loyalton, and worked at the sawmill. He lived for a couple of years in a small house in Loyalton before heading off on his own to become a rancher. In 1910, Grandpa Folchi wired back to his hometown in Premia (Piedmont), Italy, for a hometown girl he knew, Lucia Maria Sartorri. Upon her arrival, she was quickly informed by the local Swiss Italians that the name "Lucy" was an Indian name and that she should use her middle name, Maria; after that she was known as Maria, or "Mary." Giacamo (Jack) and Mary ventured out on their own in 1911, homesteading their first land purchase at the old Johnny Wood place, named after the previous owner, in Carmen Valley, Sattley, California, nestled along the west side of the majestic Sierra Valley.

Sierra Valley is the largest alpine valley in the Western Hemisphere, encompassing over 110,000 acres, about the size of Lake Tahoe. It is situated forty-five miles north of Truckee, California, and fifty miles west of Reno, Nevada. The famous renegade fur trader Jim Beckwourth made Sierra Valley's place in history when, in the 1850s, he discovered what would become Beckwourth Pass, the lowest pass in the Sierra Nevada mountain range, around the elevation of five thousand feet. Sierra Valley is ecologically known for its biodiversity in plant and animal life, spanning over two hundred square miles to include Plumas and Sierra counties. In the late 1850s after the gold rush, it is believed that many Swiss Italians moved from Reno to Sierra Valley to begin dairies and grain production due to the availability of water and its rich alluvial soils. Sierra

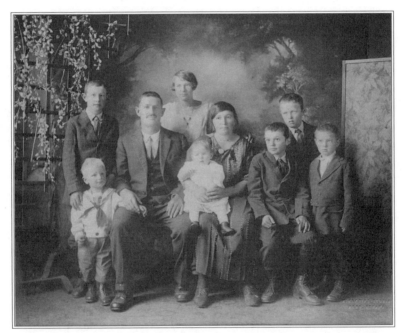

Grandma and Grandpa Folchi with their children Nina, Albert (Beno), Marion, Raymond, Emilio, Benny, and Rose.

Valley is a down-faulted basin, which in ancient times was a lake comparable to Lake Tahoe.

Around 1914, Grandma and Grandpa Folchi had their first daughter, Nina, then five boys followed: Albert (Beno), Marion, Raymond, Emilio, and Benny. My mom, Rose, was the last child born, in 1924. The family lived in Carmen Valley until 1920, when they bought the Flaherty Ranch in Beckwourth, which became their permanent residence. Giacomo ran a dairy, beef, and hay operation and milked about fifty cows a day, all by hand. My grandparents continued to buy ranches along the northwest side of Sierra Valley between the town of Beckwourth and Calpine. In all, the ranches included: the Johnny Wood Ranch, Vesti Nelson Ranch, Flaherty Ranch, and the Dr. Decker Ranch, and by 1937 the Folchis owned more than three thousand acres. The Folchis survived the Depression, and the only boys drafted for World War II were Marion and Emilio, who spent three years in Italy during the war before returning home safely. The remaining brothers, Beno, Raymond, and Benny, continued to help Grandpa until his sudden death on Thanksgiving Day in 1944.

After the war and grandpa's death, Grandma and the boys continued to work the ranches and expanded them to include cow-calf operations. Marion and Emilio got married; Marion took a job with the Plumas County road department, while Emilio worked with the brothers to carry on the ranches. The ranches now included dairy, beef cattle, hay, and grain operations. They were "working ranches"; everything was derived off the ranches. They sold milk and cream to the bigger dairies and creameries in Reno and shipped the cream by train to the Bay Area. They grew and thrashed their own grain, put up their own dryland hay, and raised their own livestock for meat production, including cattle, sheep, goats, pigs, and poultry. They also made their own products: jerky, cheese, breads, pies, sausage, bacon, canned goods, wine, and dried goods. Electricity and plumbing came into Sierra Valley in the 1940s, and that made life easier. It was said that Grandpa Folchi was the first person in Sierra Valley to have a phonograph and radio. He liked parties and was known to have everyone over for the Rocky Marciano and Joe Louis fights.

One winter around 1938, Grandpa Folchi and my uncles were out on horseback when they came upon a green pickup truck and a couple of guys cutting pine boughs from the forest. They met and had a conversation with the men, both speaking the native tongue, Italian. Instantly they became friends: Grandpa Folchi, Nonno Romano, and my dad, Louis Romano. (This became an annual event until the mid-1950s when Nonno's arthritis limited his mobility and Dad cut the boughs by himself.) The Folchis invited my dad in for lunch. Rose Folchi was very shy, and helped grandma around the ranch with the household chores and the cooking and baking for all the brothers and farm hands. She hid behind the stove when my father came in, and would periodically sneak a peek at him. Since Rose had five brothers, the word got out that she was interested in Dad, and the rest is history. Louis and Rose married in 1956, and they moved to the Redwood City flower farm next to Nonno.

The Next Generation

On December 7, 1957, the Romanos couldn't have been happier when Louis and Rose had twin boys, Larry Lodovico Romano and Gary Raymond Romano (me). The Romano workforce was in place. We were the typical Italian family at that time: "la familia" came first. Parents, kids, cousins, aunts, uncles, and grandparents all worked, ate, and socialized together. There were no exceptions. Larry and I worked side by side with Mom, Dad, and Nonno at home, on the farm, and at the flower market as soon as we could carry a bundle of flowers to the truck (at about five years old). We were expected to contribute to the family to make a living, and spent most every weekend, summer, and holiday working at the Coyote Creek

Mom and Dad cut their wedding cake.

Farm. It was tough work, but hey, we didn't know any better, and even if we did, it wouldn't have made any difference; it was the farming life.

In 1970, we got that infamous letter from Santa Clara County again: eminent domain wanted our land for a Department of Parks and Recreation scenic bike trail that would connect southern San Jose to Hellyer Park. So off went the Romanos, farther south, another fifteen miles, to purchase twenty acres in Morgan Hill, moving the farm and starting over for the last time.

The Morgan Hill flower farm steadily grew in the 1970s, until Nonno died in 1975. Larry and I were just graduating from high school, and we were tired of the farming life. We had missed out on a lot of childhood activities, like sports and school functions, because in the old Italian household everything was about work and helping the family business. After high school, I swore that I would never be a farmer, and that there must be a better life out there. Larry was interested in starting his own business, so he enrolled at College of San Mateo, and then went on to Golden Gate University in San Francisco, majoring in political science and business. I had always loved plants, nature, and the outdoors, so I also started at College of San Mateo, and then went on to Cal Poly, San Luis Obispo, majoring in horticulture and natural resources management. I finished my education with a master's degree from Chico State in recreation administration. Larry kept an active role with Mom and Dad in the flower business and supplemented his income with an antique business. I became a park ranger for San Mateo County Parks at Coyote Point Recreation Area in San Mateo in 1982. We both bought houses in Redwood City, and I helped Dad and Larry on occasional weekends and days off.

Times were changing in the cut-flower industry. During the 1980s, the United States began to open agricultural trade agreements with South America and Asia. We began to see large shipments of cut flowers—like roses, chrysanthemums, gladiolas, and carnations—from South American and Asian countries flood our flower markets, undercutting the growers in the Bay Area. Local flower growers could not compete, and by the late 1980s and early 1990s, I would estimate that 70 percent of the greenhouse growers were out of business. This took a toll on our flower business as well. Dad estimates that we lost 80 percent of our wholesale flower-shipping business, which was the majority of our income. On top of that, giants like Kmart and grocery chains were selling a lot of cut flowers in their grocery stores, and we lost another 80 percent of our retail business supplying the small florists that peppered San Francisco street corners, because they could not compete with these super grocery stores and were going out of business.

The flower farm could no longer support three Romano families, so I gave my business shares to Larry, Mom, and Dad. The business could no longer support the farm because the flower industry had been reduced to housewives coming in to buy cheap flowers and a few retail florists. In 1995, the Romano family decided to sell the twenty-acre flower farm in Morgan Hill so that Dad, Mom, and Larry could live comfortably in retirement. Sadly, Larry was diagnosed with stomach cancer in 1995 and passed away in 1997. Dad and Mom continued going to the flower market two days a week, cutting flowers off the old farm and traveling the roadsides collecting and selling wild cut flowers until 2011.

It all came to a close in the summer of 2011. Dad, now eighty-five, said: "Well, Gary, it's time. I'm giving up the stall that Nonno started at the flower market ninety-one years ago."

"Are you okay with that?" I asked.

"It's time."

Today, Dad and Mom still cut flowers along the roadsides and from their yard in Redwood City and sell them to the outside stores at the San Francisco flower market. It's in his blood to continue his business. I'm sure Dad will go down with a pruner in his hand someday.

Gary and Larry at the flower farm.

The Sierra Valley ranches were in full operation until 1964, when my grandmother died. The brothers continued ranching through the 1960s and into the 1970s, but times were changing there, too. Large corporate farms were buying out all the small farms. The local dairies began closing in Sierra Valley around the 1950s because the railroads discontinued the service of delivering cream down to Oakland and San Francisco and shipped only freight as they do today. By the late 1960s the dairies were all dried up. After the closing of the dairies, most of the Sierra Valley ranching operations became cow-calf, beef cattle, and hay operations.

Tragedy struck the Folchis in the mid-1970s when the youngest son, Uncle Benny, died while logging. A few years later, Uncle Raymond died of a sudden heart attack on the ranch, and then Uncle Beno went into a deep depression and ended up spending the rest of his life in a convalescent home. The only ones left to run the ranches were Emilio, his wife, Betty, and their sons Jack and David. Uncle Marion later retired from the Plumas County road department and he and his wife, Linda, moved to Reno. Emilio and Betty could not run the ranches by themselves, so they began selling the ranches off little by little. The first to go was the Carmen Valley Ranch (Grandpa's first ranch); next was the Vesti Nelson Ranch; then the Flaherty Ranch (where Mom was born); and by 1980 all that was left was the sixty-five-acre Dr. Decker Ranch, where Emilio and Betty lived.

In a matter of twenty years, the Folchi ranches were reduced from more than three thousand acres to only sixty-five acres. Emilio and Betty's children, Jack and David, had gone off to college. Jack graduated from Santa Clara University and landed a major job with Hewlett-Packard in the Bay Area; David graduated from San Francisco State University with a degree in communications and began working for AT&T in Oakland. By 1989 Emilio and Betty wanted to move "to town"; the ranch was too much for them to handle. That's how I got into the picture, when I received a phone call.

"Hello, Gary, this is Betty. Emilio and I have put up the ranch here in Beckwourth for sale; David and Jack aren't interested. Do you want to buy it?"

I had a decision to make. After swearing that I would never become a farmer after what Larry and I went through as children, growing up in a hardworking Italian family, did I want to give up my successful career in parks and recreation and go back to farming?

Chapter 2
GROWING UP ON THE FARM

Only he can understand what a farm is, what
a country is, who shall have sacrificed part of
himself to his farm, or country, fought to save
it, struggled to make it beautiful. Only then
will the love of farm or country fill his heart.

~Antoine de Saint-Exupéry

Did I really want to go back to farming? In a blur, thirty years scrolled quickly through my head, with me trying to pull pieces together, like movie clips—so many experiences that I want to remember, and had never thought too much about before then. My earliest memory was sitting on the old 1958 Ford tractor under the lean-to in the backyard. I was about six years old, and I remember Dad running toward me and yelling, "What the hell are you doing?" I didn't think I did anything wrong; I just started the tractor, that's all. What kid wouldn't try and start the tractor if the key was left in it?

From then on, the stories just kept rolling. I laugh at them now, but at the time, my brother Larry and I hated every minute of life on the farm. Take, for example, the last day of school. Most kids are excited, because *it's summer!* Time for playing, camping, and hanging out at the YMCA pool with your friends.

Not the Romano boys.

"Come home right away; we have to pack and get ready to go to the ranch," Dad would say on the last day of school.

We knew what we were in for: work at home, work on the "ranch" (what Dad called the Coyote Creek Farm), and work at the flower market. It started around the summer of 1964, and continued every summer through 1976.

Gary and Larry in the tractor in Redwood City.

A typical summer week for the Romano boys went like this: Monday, Wednesday, and Friday we were up at 2:15 a.m. and out the door to the flower market in San Francisco to sell, wrap, and deliver flowers until 9 a.m. We ate breakfast, returned home, watered the yard, fed the pets, did chores around the house, helped Grandpa, had dinner, relaxed, watched one hour of TV, and played with pets or rode our bikes until dark.

Tuesday and Thursday we got up at 6 a.m., packed up the truck, and headed to San Jose to cut, weed, irrigate, and perform all farm duties until about 6 p.m. We then ate dinner and returned home, loaded the truck for market, finished our chores, and were in bed by 9 p.m.

On Saturday we attended catechism until 10 a.m., then loaded up and spent the weekend at the ranch working until Sunday night—picking flowers, pumpkins, and tomatoes, and doing whatever else needed to be done. Once home, we loaded the truck for market, ate a late dinner, and went to bed by 9 p.m., ready for Monday's routine again. This routine went on from the age of six years until we were eighteen.

"Big Blue" was our 1948 one-ton GMC truck, and Dad and Nonno built a wooden bed on the back to carry all the flowers and blossoms. The day before leaving for the ranch, Larry and I helped Dad pull the canvas over metal arches to make a canopy until it looked like a prairie schooner. He added a second "deck" halfway between, so he could carry two levels of flower buckets. The next morning we packed up, stopped by Purity Market and loaded groceries for the week. As we left for the ranch, Larry and I climbed up into the second deck of the canopy for the ride to San Jose, about forty miles away. In those days, there were no seat belts or seat belt laws. Highway 101 was called "blood alley" for a reason; the speed limit was seventy miles per hour on a two-lane highway. We didn't care, because it was cool to hang up there and look back at all the cars. People waved, truckers honked—and we wondered what they were really thinking.

For twelve years, while other kids were on vacation, that was our normal routine. Once at the ranch, we drove down a long gravel driveway between orchards of cherries, walnuts, apricots, and prunes. Larry and I were expected to hop out, unlock the gate, and run and open up the "ranch house," a homemade tin garage. That garage was an interesting place to the young mind. It housed everything: farm equipment and parts, our kitchen, and our sleeping quarters. When I was young I thought of the garage as a huge place, but when I revisited the old site twenty years later, I realized that it was only about twenty feet by forty feet. That's it! How did we all fit in there? Dad and Nonno built the garage in Cupertino and then moved it to the Coyote Creek Farm. It had a concrete floor, a kitchen table, a refrigerator, a hot plate and toaster, and an Airline twelve-inch black-and-white TV on one side; the other side of the garage had racks of tools and irrigation and tractor parts; and an old Allis-Chalmers Model M cleat track and the Ford loader sat in the back. In front of the tractors were our living quarters, a regular bed for Mom and Dad, and two aluminum folding cots for Larry and me. The garage was heated with an old potbellied stove that we got from one of the ranches in Sierra Valley, and the only bathroom was the outhouse next door.

That was the arrangement for years. All the cooking was done outside—other than an easy breakfast of cold cereal and toast, juice, and coffee—or cooked on the hot plate of the potbellied stove. Nonno and Dad had set up an outdoor kitchen. We barbequed mostly with a small grill, using only dried trimmings from our flowering peach and cherry trees. Dad and Nonno had set up two one-hundred-gallon tanks— filled by hose from the farm well—to feed wash basins that we'd use to clean dishes and our hands. All the hot water we used was heated in pots on the potbellied stove and transferred to the basins.

Each morning, Dad and Mom got up around five to start the stove, and at about six roused us kids for breakfast. Dad left

Gary and Larry picking pumpkins. (I'm sleeping on the job!)

The flower truck, Big Blue, loaded and ready to go.

early with the .410 shotgun to see if there were any jackrabbits eating the flowers (we called him Elmer Fudd). Larry and I would listen for a shot and, if we heard it, go running to the door to see if Dad was successful. If so, he'd give it to the neighboring farm workers, and they were grateful for the gift. Our job was to feed the stove with fruitwood, and after breakfast it was out to the flower fields to cut flowers all day. We'd come in around six for dinner, then Dad would go out and water for an hour or two while Larry and I helped Mom with the dishes. At night we lit the stove, read, and watched a couple hours of *Wild Kingdom, The Wonderful World of Disney,* and *The Lawrence Welk Show* before going to bed.

It was a little creepy sleeping among the tractors. Mom didn't like it much, especially one night when we had shut off the lights and in the glimmer of the black-and-white TV the shadow of a spider scurried across the floor. To our excitement, it was a tarantula, which Larry and I were happy to catch and put into a jar to save until school started a few weeks later, for show and tell. I don't think Mom ever slept great after that.

Early in summer, we spent our time with Dad preparing the soil for seeding cockscomb and celosia, asters, globe amaranth, and sunflowers. Then the real work began—moving aluminum irrigation pipes and the weeding. Oh, the weeding! About two weeks after seeding came the invasion, acres and acres of a solid weed carpet that had to be pulled by hand. Larry and I hated this time of year. The rows were one hundred and fifty feet long, three feet apart, and there were more than one hundred of them. Dad, Mom, Nonno, Larry, and I would spend eight to ten hours a day, on our hands and knees, for weeks to get rid of all of the weeds. There was a stake on either end of the row; you'd look for the little flower seedlings and pull the rest. All you saw were asses and elbows. As the flowers grew, it got easier, and we then spent hours on the old Bolens garden tractor and rototilled between the rows, then pulled furrows for flood irrigation.

The rest of the summer was spent flood irrigating the fields about once a week, with a few weeding days, and then it was time to cut flowers, more flowers, and more flowers. Endless days and into the evening, stooping and bending, cutting flowers, and coming back up, tying a bunch with rope and putting it back down in the row. When an armload was ready, you would pick the flowers up, count them, walk back to the truck, put them in a bucket of water, and mark them down in Mom's tally sheet. (She was the keeper of the farm logs.)

In the flower farm's heyday, in the 1970s and 1980s, we cut hundreds of bunches a day, coming home late at night to get the truck ready for market. Nonno lived next door to us in Redwood City, but he never stayed on any of the flower farms. He'd commute for the day to help my dad, but especially to be with us kids. It's hard to believe a small family got so much work done, and it was a lot of hard work.

We did have some fun on the ranch. As I got older, Dad let me hunt for rabbits and walk along the Coyote Creek in the morning with the new .22 rifle that he bought me for my fourteenth birthday. I hunted for squirrels, quail, and cottontails while Larry scoured the banks of Coyote Creek for old bottles and relics. Larry was the old soul between us; he was fascinated with Nonno's old stories of Italy and the Depression and got into antiques at an early age. We spent hours with Grandpa, listening to his stories. I can still see Nonno speaking in broken English as he sat in his rocking chair, with his wide-brimmed hat and Toscani cigar fumigating the patio, along with a half dozen paisanos sipping grappa or drinking wine while they ranted and raved about the Roosevelt years. Although I rolled my eyes at the old men ("not this one again!"), Larry couldn't get enough of them. Some summer afternoons, Dad and Mom cut us loose from the farm around three so that we could join the local kids from across the creek and go inner tubing, fishing, and swimming in the creek. Larry was the klutz of the family, always accident prone, and I wasn't much better. Neither of us

Larry and Gary in the flowering peach orchard.

Mom and the boys on the front porch with Nonno in Redwood City.

were very coordinated: I loved sports but wasn't very good at them, and at school they called us "Spaz and Moe," the spazmo twins. We thought it was pretty funny, and played it up. On the farm, Larry was always getting hurt by falling off a piece of equipment—a gash here, a gash there. Dad would patch him up and send him out in the field again.

Once, Larry and I were hunting for squirrels, and we came across a beautiful, grassy meadow-like lawn.

Larry said to me, "Hey let's run across."

"It doesn't look for real . . . there's something not right," I said.

"I'm going anyway," said Larry, and off and down he went, right through the grass into an open cesspool, a sewage pit. Oh the smell! Dad and I got a rope and pulled him out, threw him a bar of soap, and he spent the afternoon washing in the creek. We burned his clothes. As we used to say, "That was Larry!"

Nonno retired in 1964. Arthritis had crippled his feet and hands to the point where he didn't help us much on the ranch, but he'd still come out in the afternoons to visit in his 1962 Chevy Impala Coupe. Every Sunday, after a long day's work, Larry and I would look down that long driveway for a cloud of dust, and emerging at the garage we'd see the "blue bomber" tooting its horn. It was Nonno, and that meant we could go home early! Nonno was the kingpin of the family; what he said went, no questions asked. (I always felt sorry for Mom because he didn't like her cooking. It was "too bland"—not enough lard, garlic, or olive oil—but he did offer one compliment: "Your mom makes the best pancakes.")

The ride home to Redwood City with Nonno was always an adventure. Mom and Dad were scared to death to let us go with Nonno. He was a terrible driver, and had no patience for traffic—the worst formula for a Sunday night drive home on "blood alley." Once we got to the end of the gravel driveway, it took about five minutes to wait for a break in the seventy-mile-per-hour traffic. It seemed like an eternity to him; he would swear and shake his fist at the cars going by, until finally, with no warning, he would gun it and dart out among the masses. Larry and I white-knuckled the door handles to a chorus of honking horns, screeching brakes, and flashing high beams. We hated to look at anyone because they might flip us off or give us a death stare, so we just crouched down below the seat and laughed. We were going home; that's all we cared about. After about twenty miles down the road, Dad and Mom would pass us, probably to make sure that we were still alive.

Nonno didn't really care much for driving laws. I remember one late October evening we had just picked a load of pumpkins and had overloaded the sideboards of the 1965 Chevy pickup. It was a stick shift, the old "three-on-the-tree." Nonno got about ten miles from the ranch before his arthritis hampered his shifting ability. He said to me:

"Hey, Gary, you drive."

"Nonno, I can't drive. I'm only fourteen."

"Ah, you drive on the ranch. Drive!"

He pulled over, I slid into the driver's seat, and off I went, barely peeking over the steering wheel. About twenty minutes later, who passes me but Dad and Mom. You should have seen the look on my mom's face! I'm sure she said a few Hail Marys on the way home. I had never driven seventy miles an hour before, and now I had to try and maneuver the Marsh Road off-ramp in Menlo Park. I downshifted, but was still going too fast. As I took the curve, the load of pumpkins shifted, and the truck swayed around the turn. All I could imagine was a freeway loaded with spilled pumpkins and, boy, would I be in trouble. We made it home in one piece, Larry and Nonno still laughing about it, and we never told Dad and Mom the details. It was just another episode with Nonno. Most people thought he was a grumpy old man, but he liked us twins because we were hard workers on the farm. We usually spent Sunday nights next door with him watching All-Star wrestling. Larry and I got a kick out of him swearing at the black-and-white TV in Italian, shaking his fist at Ray Stevens, Pat Patterson,

Larry, Nonno, and Gary at Christmas.

and Kinji Shibuya. He was pretty smart, though; instead of giving us sodas that would keep us up all night, he gave us a juice glass of wine and water, about half and half. We were only ten or twelve years old, and after working on the farm all day with a little wine we were out by 8 p.m. We liked spending the night with Nonno; he was funny and a great storyteller. Sometimes we would have Sunday dinners with my cousins JoAnn and Gina from Redwood City, and Irene, Johnny, and Nina from Daly City. Nonno didn't smile much, and he would tease them because they were "city kids," especially Johnny, who was in a rock-and-roll band. Nonno called him a "whippee" (he couldn't pronounce hippie with his broken English-Italian accent). Johnny was our idol, the one that got away from the farming duties. Johnny Vernazza later went on to bigger and better things as a lead guitar player for the likes of Elvin Bishop and Norton Buffalo, and starring with Marshall Tucker, the Doobie Brothers, and the Steve Miller Band.

Nonno, along with Mom and Dad, instilled in us the value of money, and to work for what you want and pay for it yourself. Gifts were usually work-related items like matching pruning shears, hoes, and shovels, or work clothes, and that was it—even for Christmas. While our friends were getting baseball mitts, bats, and basketballs, we were getting work gloves, work boots, tools, and work clothes. Larry and I laughed it off and made up stuff that we got for Christmas to tell our friends.

Our parents paid us for the work that we did on the farm by way of giving us land to grow crops. What we harvested from our plots we could sell at the flower market. Larry and I would grow about an acre of pumpkins, tomatoes, and bell peppers at the ranch, and then help Nonno grow and pick basil, pole beans, and carrots at home. During the summer, we picked and hauled home lugs of peppers and tomatoes from the ranch every week, bagged them, and sold them to the florists. That was our money to buy school clothes and start a savings account for college.

Larry and I were always looking for new ways to make money on our own. At twelve and thirteen years old, we knew it all right, so this one time in late September, Dad came home from the flower market and said to us that all the florists were looking for fall foliage branches to put into arrangements. With that in mind, the next weekend at the ranch, we took our tomato cart down along the creek and, lo and behold, we found that the banks were filled with a beautiful auburn-colored shrub. We cut almost a truckload and brought it back to the garage where Dad was bunching flowers. We thought this finding would bring joy to the folks, but to our dismay, when Mom and Dad saw us coming their eyes bulged. Dad said,

"What the hell are you guys doing?"

Larry and I looked at each other puzzled and said, "What?" We had cut a truckload of poison oak, and boy did we get paid for it! We spent a week in bed blistered up from head to toe. The only reward for that mishap was that we got out of school for a week. We learned our lesson from then on and always got advice from Dad as to what we should cut in the wild to make money and sell at the flower market.

We were quite the entrepreneurs. We took a wagon loaded with our bagged tomatoes around the neighborhood in the evening to sell, and who wouldn't buy a few bags of tomatoes from the cute thirteen-year-old Romano boys? We were also rewarded for chores, but most didn't amount to much money. We recycled all the local newspapers by unfolding them so Dad could wrap the flowers for the florists; we were paid a penny a pound. I spent hours after school spreading newspapers and shelling dried beans, only to make ninety cents. By the time we started college, Larry and I had enough money to support ourselves all the way through and never had to get a student loan. But our biggest reward was the pets. The big benefit of growing up at the ranch was bringing home wild animals. We had them all, and Dad and Mom didn't seem to care. We caught snakes, lizards, salamanders, cottontail and jackrabbit bunnies, frogs, turtles, fish, crayfish, birds, bats, and mice. What we couldn't catch on the ranch we bought: chickens, guinea pigs, cats, dogs, and even an alligator. Larry and I were never in the house; we stayed out as long as we could just playing with our animals. The only things Dad wouldn't let us catch alive were jackrabbits and the "vermin," gophers. We did have a pet jackrabbit named Winkie, who we walked around the neighborhood on a leash. Neighborhood thugs later murdered Winkie; it got local attention in the newspaper, and we were inundated with free rabbits from the community. I had a weekly trapline on the ranch of ten to twelve gopher traps to keep them out of the flowers, and I was pretty good at it; they didn't have a chance. Plus, our dog, Reno, was "the man" on jackrabbits. He'd look down each row of flowers and stalk them until a few minutes later when we'd hear the fatal squeak. Reno had done his job, and Dad would crack a smile, another one gone. Reno was our successful Elmer Fudd.

By the end of summer, we were happy to go back to school and get a break from working. Things winded down after pumpkin season in October, but Larry and I weren't out of the woods yet. Each fall we would go for weekend drives with Mom and Dad in the big GMC. We'd head into the Santa Cruz Mountains to cut madrone, toyon, and pyracantha berries; mistletoe and cattails; and to collect pinecones for Christmas sales at the flower market. After the New Year, it was pussy willow and blossom season. From January through May we spent our evenings and weekends cutting wild and French pussy willow, forsythia, flowering quince, lilacs, and peach, almond, and cherry blossoms. Larry and I logged endless hours at the ranch, hauling bales of willow and blossoms through the mud to the truck, and then hours after school bunching them for the flower market.

The highlight of the season was during Easter, when Podesta Baldocchi Flowers in San Francisco decorated Macy's and Maiden Lane with our ten-foot peach blossom branches. Dad

Larry and Gary cutting blossoms on the Grimm Ranch.

Cutting ten-foot branches for the Macy's display.

rented a huge flatbed truck, and we'd go to San Francisco and drop off all the blossoms, then eat at a nice restaurant, and shop at Union Square! It was a big deal for us kids.

By the time we started high school in 1972, things began to change. Santa Clara County had taken us over by eminent domain again, and we had about ninety days to move. The county planned to develop a bike trail along Coyote Creek and had bought us out for the face value of the property. Larry and I were heartbroken because, even though we worked hard on that property, we were going to miss playing in the creek. Dad and Nonno found twenty acres in Morgan Hill, California, an old prune orchard that a tractor repair company had owned. For us kids it was nothing special because there wasn't a creek that we could play or fish in, but Dad and Nonno were happy because it had a huge well. The well produced over one thousand gallons a minute, and the first time they turned it on, it sent a ten-inch stream of water hundreds of feet in the air. You would have thought we struck oil or something. The Italians were jubilant! We spent the spring of 1972 moving plants and transplanting new flowering peach, cherry, and nectarine trees, as well as lilac, euonymus, pussy willow, forsythia, and flowering quince shrubs. During the winter of 1972–73, Larry and I helped Nonno graft more than two hundred fruit trees, from those that produced fruit to ornamental double-flowering trees, and helped Dad and Mom get the new farm on its feet. Larry and I never ever got attached to this farm, called the Grimm Ranch. It came with all kinds of tractors and buildings, and a "labor house," a metal building that housed the farm workers. Dad had Larry and I paint it and remodel it somewhat; we added a potbellied stove, and it had a kitchen and bathroom. But it was all metal—too hot in the summer, and too cold in the winter—and we hated it.

During high school, Larry and I found more reasons not to work on the farm. Nonno died during our junior year, Dad quit smoking and mellowed out, and Mom and Dad started giving us a little freedom. By then I was doing most of the

Preparing the Union Square display in San Francisco.

tractor work getting the fields ready for seeding, while Dad seeded and Larry was "the main man" at the flower market. Once the flowers were ready to harvest, we had to go to market on Mondays, Wednesdays, and Fridays, and go to the ranch and cut flowers Tuesdays, Thursdays, Saturdays, and Sundays. During the summer it was no picnic; it was seven days a week. I hated flower market mornings. At 2:15 a.m. the alarm went off, and Dad opened the bedroom door and said, "Okay, get up. You awake?" As soon as we said yes, he hit the lights, and Larry and I had fifteen minutes to be dressed and out the door, without breakfast. We had to help Dad load the truck, and it was off to market.

The San Francisco flower market was something else. Just like the popular TV series *The Streets of San Francisco*, and exciting like the *Dirty Harry* movies, San Francisco was booming at that time. Businesses flourished, and the gay movement was in full force by the mid-1970s and into the 1980s. The flower market was thirty minutes away, so Larry and I tried to catch a few zzz's on the way. Once we arrived, we were thrust into the bustling "city within a city." The city of San Francisco was quiet at around two thirty in the morning, but the flower market was wide awake. At Sixth and Brannan Streets, it was four blocks of hustle and bustle and flower carts going in every direction. Italians argued with Japanese and Chinese vendors, and anyone else who wanted to argue; nobody was listening. Deals, steals, and bartering took place on every corner. You'd see all walks of life at that hour, from gay and lesbian florists to old-timers, wholesale truckers, and retail wives. You could find anything to do with flowers there—fresh roses, carnations, gladiolus, cut greens, potted plants, silk and dry flowers, and everything in between. There were stores with boxes, corsages, wrapping paper, bows, vases—you name it, it was there. Every flower grower had his or her own year-round stall inside the warehouse. Our stall was twenty feet by thirty feet, and caged so that we could lock our flowers in after the market closed for the night.

Wouldn't you buy a nice bunch of flowers from these gentlemen?

Dad would back in to our stall, and Larry and I unloaded the buckets of cut flowers. While Dad took the truck out to the parking lot, our job was to start putting up the flower orders. Every florist had a retail badge number, and we put the florists' orders in small cubicles according to their badge number. All of the extra flowers were displayed on the front tables for the florists to buy. Dad and Larry had the gift of gab; why, t   here wasn't a florist that they couldn't talk into buying something. They were ruthless, like hyenas on a kill. While Larry and Dad were making a killing, my job was mostly to wrap the flowers in newspaper, put them on a cart, and deliver them to the florists' vehicles in the dark alleys around the flower market. That was a little scary, because at that hour the alleys were full of drunks, drug dealers, and shady-looking characters. I was young, around fifteen to eighteen years old, and I was a little nervous when I had to deliver flowers down those dark streets, but I just kept to myself and did my deliveries. Everyone knew we were "the Romano boys," and they didn't want to mess with Dad, so we were fine. After all the excitement, by 8 a.m., we were sold out and Dad took us to breakfast. It was a full morning of nonstop pushing, wrapping, and delivering flowers. This was religiously done on Monday, Wednesday, and Friday mornings from June through September. To compound that, during the summer months, we had so many flower orders that we would have breakfast after market, then go home, pick up Mom, and head to the flower ranch and begin cutting flowers for the next market. I never fully acclimated to the time changes—going from a 2 a.m. start to a 6 a.m. start the next day. To this day, I don't know how Dad did it for seventy-five years.

I had a lot to consider before I committed to returning to the farming life.

The Romano stall at the San Francisco flower market.

Chapter 3
MOUNTAIN MEN

I am losing precious days. I am degenerating
into a machine for making money. I am learning
nothing in this trivial world of men. I must
break away and get out into the mountains to
learn the news.

~John Muir

If I had to sum up life on the flower farm, as I remember
it, it would be intense, fast and furious, and full of action;
something was going on all the time. What made a peaceful
change of pace was going to visit my mom's side of the family,
the Folchis, who were dairy and cattle ranchers in Sierra
Valley. When you were living, working, and going to school
in the highly populated San Francisco Bay Area, going to visit
Grandma Mary Folchi and Mom's brothers in Sierra Valley was
a treat. The wide-open, 220-square-mile alpine valley seemed
like a different planet compared to the Bay Area. Why, there
were more people in Redwood City than all of Plumas and
Sierra counties combined. It was a totally different experience.

The Folchis ranched three-thousand-plus acres, and it
was all about cattle, horses, sheep, pigs, goats, and chickens,
and milking, haying, hunting, and ranching. Not flowers,
anything but flowers! My earliest memory from my time in
the mountains is of Grandma Mary getting mad at Larry for
touching something on the stove. She was a short, somewhat
fat lady with rosy cheeks. She was the boss of all my uncles,
Beno, Marion, Raymond, Emilio, and Benny. That's about all
I remember, because she died in 1964 when Larry and I were
seven years old. We went up to visit every year at the end of hay
season (Labor Day), and for Thanksgiving, so Dad could cut

The Folchi mountain men: Benny, Raymond, Beno, and Blue Boy the dog (t) and Emilio, Raymond, and Benny at the Nelson Ranch (b).

pinecone boughs—this was a full-day event. For Thanksgiving, we packed up "Big Blue," the GMC one-ton, and started out at about four in the morning. We stopped at Denny's for breakfast in Roseville, and maybe to see our cousins Barbara and Jim Avila there, then continued on to the ranch, which I live on today. My uncles would greet us, as did a surround sound of horses grunting, pigs snorting, chickens cackling, cows mooing, sheep baaing, goats head-butting each other, and "Blue Boy," the dog, barking. He was always waiting to greet us at the car door.

It was a relaxing feeling to arrive because Larry and I knew the uncles weren't going to put us to work. They invited us kids in the morning to help them on their daily chores, but it was different, and it never felt like work. They were real "mountain men." Most of the uncles (Beno, Raymond, Emilio, and Benny) came in for breakfast around nine in the morning, after being out milking or feeding the animals starting at four. They were rough looking, with leatherlike skin and layers of worn clothing, each wearing a distinguishable hat. They would come in and discuss the day's activities, and schedule them over breakfast, which usually consisted of eggs, bacon, sausage, pancakes, and coffee. Everything but the coffee came from the ranch. It was fascinating to hear Mom and her brothers talk about the early years with Grandpa Folchi, and their survival stories about being only eleven and twelve years old and getting stranded for weeks at another ranch ten miles away because of a twelve-foot snowfall from a huge blizzard that shut down Sierra Valley. These people were tough; no wimps allowed! I think about what life was like then: no plumbing, no electricity. All you had was leather and wool clothing, and woodstoves for heat. Water was taken from shallow, hand-dug wells with a hand pump and windmills. The bathroom was an old "two-seater" outhouse. I guess when it was twenty below zero and you had to go, it didn't matter who was in there. Either way, at twenty below zero you weren't going to stay in there very long!

The uncles went out twice a day during the winter months to milk fifty cows and feed them hay and break ice to give them water, moving five to six feet of snow along the way. Mom told stories about how they got so much snow that the pigs would make tunnels, and all you saw were their little eyes peeking out. It was a hard life, but that's just what you did in those days. All the hot water was heated on the stove and poured into basins to wash your face and hands. You maybe took a bath once a week. That's it. There were no radio, TV, or weather forecasts; you didn't know when the storms were coming, where they would hit, or how long they would stay! The Folchis entertained themselves with reading, musical instruments, dancing, and socializing. They all played the guitar, harmonica, or accordion (all Italians have to have an accordion player in the family), and they danced to the polkas and music from Hank Williams, Dean Martin, and Frank Sinatra. Travel was done by horse and buggy, sleds in the winter, and later on, the Ford Model T and Model A. There were no paved roads, so the early narrow-wheeled vehicles got stuck in the mud. The Folchis went back to horseback, until the 1940s, when asphalt roads came to Plumas County.

Your life depended on the ranches and everything came from the land. There were no supermarkets, convenience stores, or Home Depots. All you had was the Sears, Roebuck and Company catalog. The Folchis did everything: they raised goats, chickens, lambs, pigs, cows, and horses. They milked cows and goats, drank raw milk and cream, and made their own cottage cheese, ricotta, yogurt, and other cheeses. They butchered all their own meats—chicken, lamb, goat, pig, and cattle—and ate everything "off of the hoof," from prime rib and London broil to pig's feet, cow brains, heart, liver, sweetbreads, and tongue. They lived off of not only the domestic animals but from wild animals as well. The family trapped coyotes, minks, beavers, muskrats, bobcats, raccoons, and badgers to sell their pelts; hunted quail, grouse, duck, geese, deer, rabbit, and squirrel; and fished for trout, bass, catfish, carp, and crayfish for food. To keep things fresh in the summer, they got ice from ice companies in the area, who used horses and special plows to cut blocks of

A little bit of snow doesn't bother the cows in Sierra Valley.

ice from ice ponds during the winter and then stored them in icehouses throughout the summer. (You kept things fresh by buying ice blocks and putting them in your icebox.) Long-term storage items like onions, garlic, potatoes, salami, jerky, canned goods, dried fruits, and hard cheeses were kept in root cellars that were dug below ground. What they couldn't get from the ranches, they brought up from the Central Valley. Grandma had transient ranch hands that were homeless from the Depression, the War, or "just passing through," who would work the hay season, many times for just room and board. Visitors would also come up from San Francisco for deer-hunting season. In return, they brought fruits and vegetables, grapes, wine, and whiskey to barter for being able to deer hunt the three thousand acres, or work for food. Grandma and Mom spent hours cleaning fish, processing meats, baking, and putting up canned and dried goods for the winter. In addition, Grandma, Dena (Mom's oldest sister), and Mom weaved and knitted their own clothes and planted the gardens. Grandpa and the uncles built all their own fences, outbuildings, and barns from lumber that came from local mills, and fabricated all hitches, hinges, and fittings from blacksmithing.

I can remember at dinnertime on the ranch, after the uncles had some brandy and a few glasses of wine, the stories flowed like a river. Larry and I sat for hours listening, and the more Dad laughed, the more the stories came and the louder they got. They were all great storytellers. Uncle Beno scared us kids at bedtime telling us not to go outside at night because "the mountain lion" would get us. He was the oldest brother, never married, and accident prone; he had mowed one of his toes off with a lawn mower, and supposedly chopped off his thumb with an axe and the rooster ran off with it. He was the milker, welder, and main ranch hand as well as the accordion player and "teaser," always teasing the animals and us kids. Then there was Uncle Raymond; he was our favorite. The best storyteller, tall and thin, easygoing, and good looking, with his distinctive old cowboy hat, he also never married but was the baker and gardener and tended the sheep and goat herd. He wrote us letters, sent us care packages of sausage and cheeses for the holidays, and took us out hunting and fishing. Uncle Emilio worked on the neighboring ranch with his wife, Betty, and their two kids, Jack and David. My cousin Jack was five years older than Larry and me, so we mostly hung out with David; he was our age. Emilio was the hunter in the family, he had fought in World War II, and was the brains of the ranches as far as operations and technical skills in carpentry, mechanics, fabricating, electrical, and plumbing. I remember Emilio riding a big white horse, and always deer hunting.

The big event on the ranches was opening day of deer season, when most of the uncles, their neighbors, and other relatives would come over early in the morning and get their assignment from Emilio as to where they would be positioned along the mountainside. The objective was to run the deer across the mountainside to allow the hunters to get a good shot. Emilio was the best shot of all the hunters; Uncle Beno and cousin Albert were good too, but Emilio never missed. If the deer was standing or running, no matter what the distance, if it was in Emilio's crosshairs, a clean kill, a fatal shot to the neck, was inevitable. They preached "a clean, humane kill" or to not take the shot. There was no trophy hunting, no hunting for sport. Even though they enjoyed hunting, it was all about the care of the meat. Taking a bad shot would ruin the shoulder, or the hindquarters. They wanted the quick kill because the more an animal was stressed, the tougher the meat. Emilio gave me my first deer rifle, a .257 Roberts that was his prized deer rifle, at sixteen years old. (I still use it to this day, but I'm by no means in the same class of shooters as Emilio.)

Uncle Benny was "the bull" of the uncles, though he was the youngest. "Strong as an ox," they called him. He was short, square, and jolly, always laughing. He was the horseman, the guitar player, and along with working the ranches with his brothers, he was a logger. Also a single man, he would come in at night from logging all covered in forest soot, just the whites of his eyes peeking out, with a bright smile. He was always the nicest-dressed uncle, with starched collars, new jeans, fancy boots, and a big silver Western belt buckle. The last brother was Marion, the second oldest, another thin man and great storyteller. He left the ranches after World War II to work for the Plumas County road department. Marion and his wife, Linda, and their two daughters, Kathy and Virginia, lived in the town of Beckwourth, a couple of miles from the ranch. Every summer, we would come up to the ranches for about a week around Labor Day and hang out with our cousins David, Virginia, and Marie. David was the son of my uncle Emilio and Aunt Betty, and Virginia was the daughter of Uncle Marion and Aunt Linda. Marie was an adopted cousin to Virginia (yeah, these Italian families go on and on and on). We'd get into mischief, and laugh for hours at the stupidest things and the weird people of Sierra Valley. It was always a fun time, having great Labor Day picnics up at the Nelson Ranch, back in the canyons. The uncles would play music, yodel, and get a little tipsy while we rode our minibikes and played in the woods.

Going to the ranches every summer and Thanksgiving and seeing the uncles was a special time for me because I loved talking to them, being outdoors, hiking, hunting, and fishing. I wanted to be the mountain men that they were, and live off the land. From high school on, I was into hiking, hunting, and fishing. I even learned to tan hides, and mail ordered a taxidermy course from Northwestern School of Taxidermy in Nebraska to learn how to stuff animals. I was intrigued by how the North American Indians survived off the land, and started to learn about edible and medicinal plants. On my travels with Mom and Dad cutting wildflowers, I began to identify them in the countryside and realized that was what I wanted to learn about in college.

After Nonno died in my junior year of high school, Dad and Mom actually pushed us to get a college education. Since no one in our family had ever gone to college, Larry and I jumped at the opportunity. Researching college degrees, I found that natural resources management would encompass all of my interests: the outdoors, plants and animals, and the environment. As I attended College of San Mateo, and then Cal Poly, San Luis Obispo, parks and recreation just seemed like a good fit for me. After college, I accepted a park ranger job back in my hometown county of San Mateo. I was excited to get a good-paying job in my field. I climbed the ranks very quickly, and after a few years the county officials started grooming me to be the future parks and recreation director.

But the hustle and bustle of city life and the congested Bay Area was getting old. I wanted to live in the open air of the mountains and get away from it all. I was spending all my weekends running up "the hill" to the Sierra to fish, hike, or hunt, so I began keeping my eyes open for park jobs near Sierra Valley. Finally in 1988, a job opened up for park superintendent at Tahoe City Public Utility District, and before I knew it I was packing up my belongings and moving to Tahoe City on New Year's Eve, with Mom and Larry helping me. We rang in the New Year at the Gold Spike Saloon in Tahoma, in a blizzard, with everything I owned packed in Dad's two-wheel-drive pickup, complete with its high box for flowers. Mom didn't drink much, but she was putting away the brandies that night because she and Larry thought I was nuts for giving up the great job with San Mateo County. Larry really never liked hunting or fishing or the outdoors much; he was a city dweller. He loved to dress up and go to vaudeville-like parties, where you dressed and danced to the music of twenties, thirties, and forties.

Larry was at home in San Francisco. "For me, camping is staying at a Motel 6," he'd say.

Looking back through it all, my childhood was a positive one—one that made me who I am today. But now, I had to decide: Did I want to be a farmer?

Chapter 4
THE METAMORPHOSIS OF A
SMALL ORGANIC FARMER

... no other human occupation opens so wide a
field for the profitable and agreeable combination
of labor with cultivated thought, as agriculture.
~Abraham Lincoln

As I held the phone in silence, I thought for a minute about what my Aunt Betty had just offered me, the last piece of the family farm. In a spur-of-the-moment reaction, I answered in an unsure voice: "Yeah . . . sure, I'll buy it."

Betty said, "Okay, let's get together. I'll get the paperwork." After I hung up, I took a walk along the west shore of Lake Tahoe. I was excited, but scared about the decision I had just made. I spent an hour thinking of all the great memories on that ranch in Sierra Valley as a kid, but was afraid of giving up my wonderful fifteen-year career in parks and recreation. Not only was I afraid to give up that secure paycheck with health benefits but going off on my own felt risky. I had been away from the farming business for over fifteen years, and while I was growing up I was under my father's wing. This time I would be on my own. What would I even grow? What grew in Sierra Valley? What were my brother, Larry, and my folks going to say when I told them I was buying the last sixty-five acres of the Folchi Ranch? Was I NUTS? Larry, of all people, would think I was crazy—he knew firsthand how much we hated all that hard work farming as a kid. Did I really want to go back to that? Maybe I needed my head examined!

That night in 1989, I called my folks to tell them the news. I held the phone at arm's length as my mom said, "WHAT? You're going to throw all your education and a good job out the window and go back to pulling weeds? Are you crazy? You left the farm to get away from all that."

"Yes, Mom, that's right!"

Mom and Dad never said a discouraging word again about it, and to this day they have been my biggest supporters. I think they knew that I was meant to go back to the earth, just like Dad and my grandfather.

As I reminisced about my childhood on the flower farm and the Sierra Valley ranches, I felt the pull of my farming heritage. I was at a point in my parks-and-recreation career that the next step was to become a director, a suit-and-tie guy—sitting at a desk, pushing paper, and kissing ass to the general public and political officials. That wasn't me! Like it or not, I'm a blue-collar guy. As most of my close friends would say, "Romano belongs in Sierra Valley on that ranch—that's Romano."

There began my quest to save this family farm, my way, not anyone else's. I had some guilt when I left for college and then took a career in parks and recreation that I had abandoned my family on the flower farm. In hindsight it didn't matter because Mom, Dad, and Larry ended up selling the farm in 1995 anyway. I wondered, if only had I stayed, would we have been able to save the farm? Upon a later discussion with Dad, I discovered that wasn't the case; he said there were just too many changes in the flower industry that caused the loss of the flower farm.

"When you kids were small in the 1960s and '70s, the flower market was full of small flower growers from the Peninsula and Half Moon Bay that grew all the flowers for the flower market, and most were sold locally and shipped all over the country. Then, in the '80s and '90s as the cost of land and utilities went up, it became too expensive to produce flowers in greenhouses, so companies began to move to Mexico and South America because it was more affordable. That was the major decline of the local growers; little by little we all went out of business," he said. "Even us, that's why we sold in 1995."

So with a clear conscience, I wasn't going to let the last of the Folchi ranch slip away. I met with Betty and Emilio and signed the papers:

SOLD: To Gary Romano. OCCUPATION: Farmer.

The next weekend I traveled one hour from my house on the west shore of Lake Tahoe to the ranch in Plumas County, on County Road A23 in Beckwourth. No one was home, so I walked around the property, exuberant about the rundown and "Peter-tumble-down"—a phrase Mom would use to describe broken-down shacks or buildings—sixty-five-acre ranch that I had bought. I walked to every outbuilding, sixteen in all, painted in a dull, whitewash red. They were all there as I remembered them: the bunkhouse, the chicken coop, the pig shed, the granary, the hay barn, the dairy, the "slaughter salon," the two-seater outhouse, the toolshed, both well houses, the shop, the tractor shed, the calving lean-to, and the house and garage, each with distinct memories. The ranch didn't even have a shovel on it because Emilio and Betty had auctioned off all the equipment and tools one year before. I didn't care; I was like a pig in shit, happier than a clam. I had a piece of the ranch, broken fences and all, that I could now call mine.

I didn't think much of what I was going to do with the ranch; I was just going to enjoy it. I stayed at Lake Tahoe and visited the ranch on my days off, just hiking around Sierra Valley, going fishing and hunting, and having barbecues and parties there.

In 1990, I decided to move to the ranch and commute to my job in Tahoe City, which was an hour's drive. I would stay with Tahoe friends sometimes during the week to ease the commute, but I knew this commuting business wasn't going to work in the long run. Plus, in my mind, I was a farmer now. I'd better start farming.

It was time to figure out what I could do with the ranch. Sixty-five acres was too small to start a livestock operation. I remembered animals were a full-time job for my uncles because of the hard winters in Sierra Valley, so that wasn't an option. I wasn't into horses, cattle, or any livestock; they just seemed to be a pain in the ass to deal with anyway. One thing that I was interested in was native plants. While I was at Cal Poly in San Luis Obispo, I became curious about how the American Indians used native plants for food, how to identify native plants, and how to incorporate them into the landscape. For my senior-year project, I self-published *A Hiker's Guide to Wild Edible Plants of San Luis Obispo County*, in 1982. While I was a park ranger for San Mateo County Parks at Coyote Point Recreation Area, I put on numerous native plant walks and talks, so after a long, cold, snowy winter on the ranch in 1990, I decided to start a native plant nursery. The metamorphosis had begun: transforming the ranch to a farm and a park superintendent back to a farmer. Sierra Valley Wholesale Nursery was born in 1990, a small nursery dedicated to propagating and selling native plants for the Sierra Nevada mountain range. A park superintendent job came up with the Truckee-Donner Recreation and Park District in Truckee, California, and I got the job. Truckee was only a forty-five-minute commute, and I negotiated a company truck for the drive. This made it reasonable for me. I could now get serious about building a nursery on the farm.

In late 1990, I put together a business plan and was able to secure an $80,000 loan through Plumas Corporation to finance a heated-propagation greenhouse (1,200 square feet), two solar cold frames (3,600 square feet), a shade house (40 by 120 square feet), and drilling a well. Now I had to build them. After starting my new job in Truckee, I didn't have any vacation time, nor was I very good at construction; most of my limited talent was rough "ranch construction." I looked to my friends for help. My buddy Rob, a known partner in crime and my past roommate at Chico State, was a contractor and out of work, so I said, "Hey Rob, can I hire you to build the greenhouses?"

The project was on! Rob was known for being a great carpenter; that was his trade. He worked diligently through the summer of 1991 to build all three greenhouses. He endured the wind, cold, and heat of Sierra Valley and perfectly assembled a truck-and-trailer load of nuts and bolts. It was a massive erector set, to say the least. The only flaw through it all was the assembly of the last and most difficult greenhouse, the A-frame design, built with state-of-the-art rigid polycarbonate panels with all the bells and whistles and designed to withstand eighty-mile-per-hour winds with an eighty-pound snow load. It would have an automated temperature control for heating, ventilation, and humidity, and hydronic heating in the propagation beds. This greenhouse would be used to propagate our native plants from seed and cuttings. It had prefabricated trusses with end collars that had to fit perfectly over steel four-by-four posts. The spacing had to be perfect.

On the day of truth, when all was in place, we loaded all eight of the trusses on the top of my old '66 dump truck; it was just the right height to back in and slide the trusses onto the posts. The day was incredible; each truss slipped perfectly onto the posts. At about four thirty in the afternoon we rejoiced as the last truss went on without a hitch: "PARTY! PARTY! PARTY!" It was "beer thirty!" We closed up the end, and the final greenhouse was DONE! To my surprise, the next morning while I was at my parks office in Truckee, I got a call from Rob.

"Hey, have you seen the dump truck?"

"No, it must be by the greenhouse," I said.

A moment of silence passed between us.

"Oh shit, did we close it in the greenhouse last night?"

Yes, we did. Through the excitement (and maybe a few early beers), we had closed in the end of the greenhouse, forgetting that the dump truck was inside—now that's Italian! Rob soon cut out the front, and drove the dump truck out, then reclosed it. It was a great ending to a great project. I was now in business.

The period between 1991 through 1993 was an unsettling time, a transition period for me. A lot of things happened so fast and in every direction: I got married, had a wonderful baby daughter, moved to a new place, got a new job, and started a side business on the farm (Sierra Valley Wholesale Nursery). On top of that, my brother was diagnosed with a terminal disease, and I then got a divorce and split the family. It was too much, too fast. I admit that I didn't handle a lot of things right, but it is what it is. Shit happens, and you live with it. Despite it all, I was able to keep the farm. I knew then that my heart was not in parks and recreation and that I wanted to go back and work the farm. I knew I was born to farm.

The greenhouses were done, Sierra Valley Wholesale Nursery was born, and it was time to see if I could make a living off of the farm. I continued to commute to my parks job in Truckee, using all my vacation time and income to build the nursery business. After a couple of years, I realized that my business plan looked only good on paper. In the real world, projected and promised government contracts were nowhere to be found, and my nursery business was in no way going to support the family, let alone my $100,000 capital investment. As a matter of persistence and stubbornness to keep the farm, and as a matter of survival, I decided to add a landscape element, Lake Level Environments, to the nursery to use my native plants. Since they weren't selling, I had quite a surplus. From 1992 to 1995 it was just me, myself, and I trying to cover a park job, run a nursery, and do landscaping on the side. I was putting in seventy to eighty hours a week, and it was ridiculous. Something had to change. The whole point of buying the ranch was to someday make a living off of the farm, but I was never home, so how could I enjoy the farm if I was gone all the time? It was a catch-22. I needed to work the parks and landscape jobs to support the nursery, but it took me away from the farm. So now what?

Around 1993 my boss, Steve Randall at Truckee-Donner Recreation and Park District, asked me to find a location within our parks for a Truckee farmers' market. At that time Highway 267 was the old Brockway Highway, so I located the farmers' market at the Truckee River Regional Park. It was an instant success. On opening day I remember we had about one dozen growers, a small market, but everyone was excited—the farmers *and* the patrons. Farmers' markets were a new trend starting all over in the Sierra. The parking lot was full, there were fruit growers, a strawberry grower from Watsonville, an olive oil vendor, but the one that caught my eye was an organic vegetable grower from outside of Oroville. I was curious about all the hype over "organic." What is organic? I asked the grower, Sharon, and she went into detail about growing vegetables with just manures, composts, and cover cropping, and not using anything man-made, fertilizers, or pesticides. That night on my drive home, my wheels began spinning, and I said to myself, "Hmmm . . . farmers' market . . . flower market; vegetables . . . flowers; empty corrals . . . years of composted animal manure . . . THAT'S IT!" I learned how to grow flowers as a child with Dad and Nonno; I would just grow vegetables instead, and do farmers' markets. I quickly staged into a new form of my metamorphosis, which was to replace the landscape business with vegetable production. I could now stay home and work the farm and nursery.

Things began to move forward. I had met a new girl, Kim Schauer, around that time, and we married and began to make plans for a future on the farm. The next step was to figure out what the hell I could grow in the harsh Sierra Valley environment. I remembered that Nonna and Uncle Raymond were the gardeners, and behind the bunkhouse they had a great garden of lettuces, carrots, potatoes, and rhubarb. So I thought I'd start with that and expand on cool-season crops, those you would find growing in the winter anywhere else. Every Tuesday at the Truckee farmers' market, I would stroll through to see what the farmers were bringing. None of them farmed above three thousand feet in elevation; they were mostly from Sacramento Valley, or the foothills around Auburn, California, an elevation below two thousand feet. The farmers' market ran from June through the end of September, and I realized the farmers' crops were all warm-season varieties like corn, tomatoes, cucumbers, squash, and of course all the fruit crops like peaches, apricots, plums, and pluots. I knew I couldn't grow fruit trees because of our harsh winters and June frosts, but there wasn't a leaf of lettuce anywhere in the market by late July. A light bulb went off. "That's it!" I'll grow winter vegetables in the summer. I know how to do farmers' markets because I've done the flower market with Dad and Larry for years, so that's what I'll do.

But how would I do it? I didn't really have any farm tools or implements, or time off from parks and recreation. All I had was a Bobcat skid-steer loader for landscaping and snow removal, and I needed to make a decision about my future. Was it time to consider a career change for good? I decided in 1996 that it was time to sink or swim in the farming business. This half-ass way of supporting the farm with my parks job and supplementing it with a little nursery and landscape money wasn't the way to go. Shit or get off the pot—that's me. I've never been one to do things conservatively; it's all or nothing, and ALL it was. I jumped in with both feet; I was now a full-time farmer. I was determined to support the farm and my family one way or another with income generated from the farm.

In Redwood City, around 1995, Larry and Dad had decided that the flower farm in Morgan Hill was too much for them to handle and that the flower business had declined to the point that it wasn't worth keeping the farm. Urban sprawl had taken over Morgan Hill, and the land prices had skyrocketed. My folks could sell the twenty-acre farm to a developer for twenty times what they had bought it for in 1970. I had a 10 percent share in the business, and Dad asked me, "Do you want money or the equipment?" As I had no farm equipment, it was more valuable to me to take all the tractors, implements, irrigation pipes, and the like because I knew how to operate and use all of the equipment. The tractors were the old Model M Allis-Chalmers, cleat tracks, and wheel tractors, nothing new by any means, but I could now focus on farming my vegetables. In surveying the property, the best land for vegetables was all the old corrals that had fifty-plus years of manures, about six acres in all. It was prime, silty clay loam, rich and deep, virtually virgin over the last twenty-five years. I couldn't wait to dig in. I gave my notice to Truckee-Donner Recreation and Park District in late 1996, and helped them find my replacement into 1997. By the summer of 1997, my seventeen-year career in parks and recreation was over. My metamorphosis was almost complete. I was back to where I belonged, to the farm, and would never look back. Now I had to prove to myself and to my family that I could make a living as a farmer like my dad and my grandparents did. The pressure was on.

Kim and I were married in 1996, and our son, Joey, was born in 1998. Kim had left her job in Truckee too, and now we were focused on the farm. I was extremely nervous at the start. I cashed out my retirement to drill a needed well and purchase more equipment and supplies to establish the farm. During the 1997 season I saw how incredible our vegetables grew—lettuces, radishes, beets, spinach, carrots, broccoli, and cabbage, without any fertilizers or amendments. I knew I could grow them organically just like Dad and Nonno had grown the cut flowers in San Jose. The organic industry was just getting into mainstream America, so I contacted our local organic certifier, California Certified Organic Farmers (CCOF), and after reviewing the organic standards I realized that growing organically was just the way the old Italians farmed anyway. It was a slam dunk. We were certified organic in 1999, and our first year selling organic produce was in 2000. The fields began producing an incredible quality of organic vegetables because of our cool nights and rich soils. I just had to figure out what to do with it all. How would I sell it, and who was going to buy it?

I began signing up for all the local farmers' markets that were available in Truckee, Tahoe City, and Reno. At the time we started growing vegetables, the landscape business and native plant nursery accounted for 90 percent of our income, which wasn't enough to support us. In order to give up the landscape business, vegetable production would have to really pick up the deficit. That meant I had to sell a shitload of produce. I called a produce distributor friend of mine, Bob Habeger, in Carnelian Bay, and told him that I was now a farmer and had organic vegetables available for him to sell to his customers. He asked for a list and said he would get back to me. Shortly after, I got a call from Chef Mark Estee, from Moody's Bistro and Lounge in Truckee, saying that he talked to Bob about tying in with a local farmer to provide fresh, sustainable, organic produce to the restaurant for an article in the *Tahoe Quarterly*. Mark said, in his heavy Boston accent, "Hey Gary, how about I come to the farm, cook you and your wife dinner, and we talk about what you can grow for us?"

Thinking not too much would come of it, I said, "Sure, come on out and let's talk."

A couple of days later, a white van rolled up to the house, the side door popped open, and Mark and his sous-chef hopped out and came to our front door with a platter of salmon and four or five bottles of expensive wine. I looked at my wife, Kim, and said, "I think native plants are going out the window—we are now in the produce business!" From that day on, organic vegetables became our main focus, and we supplemented them with our native plants. Today about 85 percent of our business is organic produce with only 15 percent coming from our native plant nursery.

The metamorphosis of this farmer was complete. It was full speed ahead.

Sierra Valley Farms – three generations later, it's still in the family!

Chapter 5
WHERE HAVE ALL THE SMALL FARMERS GONE?

The farmer is the only man in our economy
who buys everything at retail, sells everything
at wholesale, and pays the freight both ways.
~John F. Kennedy

Every year we lose thousands of small farmers across America, and it's not getting any better. Staggering statistics came out of the last USDA Agricultural Census Study (2002–2007). (The next USDA Agricultural Census is due out anytime, and surely the figures haven't improved.) Take a look:

- The average age of farmers rose to fifty-seven years of age.
- Farmers over the age of seventy-five grew by 20 percent.
- Farmers under the age of thirty decreased by 30 percent.
- For each farmer under thirty-five there are six over sixty-five.
- Only 35 percent of all farms say farm income is their primary source of income.

In addition, American farms peaked in 1935 with about seven million farms then had a steady decline over the years to just over two million in 2011.

Folks, this is not good news. Where have all the farmers gone? It's pretty easy to see that the old-timers are holding on to their farms longer because, one, as with my family, there is no one interested in taking them over and, two, the young people can not afford to go into farming because it's too expensive to get started and you can't make any money doing it. Something is wrong with this picture.

As a third-generation farmer, I've seen my family alone go through eminent domain, economic hardships, family tragedies, and the loss of markets due to industrial and factory farming and import of commodities from other countries. We have lost a family farm and saved a family ranch.

Over the last century, I believe what has contributed to the decline in the number of small farmers is the takeover of small farms by large corporate factory farms, media's impact on Western society, and the development of high technology electronics.

To start, today's industrial agriculture consists of industrial farming practices and factory farms. Industrial farming began after World War II, when a surplus of petroleum chemicals used during the war, such as ammonium nitrate and ammonium sulfate, were found to have a nutrient value in agriculture for nitrogen, phosphorus, and potassium, the major nutrient base of all plants. Thanks to technological advances, farmers could use bigger, sophisticated equipment, along with cheap chemicals to vastly expand their operations. The industrial farming revolution was on—thus the slogan in the 1960s, "Get big or get out." So farms got bigger and the concept of monoculture (growing one large crop) began to take over the US and world markets. Factory farms relate mostly to livestock. The principle is the same, and factory farms also began in the 1960s, based on the industrial farming concept, which is to raise and produce meat and dairy products in a similar fashion as an assembly line creating widgets. It's based on density and production per square foot. These two ways of industrial farming led to the demise of small family farms because large corporate farms could now grow large amounts of agricultural commodities (corn, soybeans, cotton, wheat, and rice) more efficiently and with more productivity per acre than ever before. Due to the world's demand for these commodities, these large corporations began to receive subsidies from the US government to keep the prices cheap enough for the world's markets. Through the use of monocropping and applying cheap petroleum-based fertilizers, industrial farming practices could farm at a lower cost than the small family farmers and it soon began running the small family farms out of business.

Next came the age of television and the media's impact on Western society, which portrayed a negative image of the small American farmer. In the 1960s, the development of TV allowed the media to explode. People were entertained by television. Shows like *I Love Lucy* and *Leave It to Beaver* depicted the American male as a movie star and the good life as that of the white-collar worker. The blue-collar worker was someone looked down on, and someone to make fun of, holding an occupation that you would be embarrassed to say you had. "I'm a farmer" was not an inspiring statement you'd want to broadcast. TV shows like *The Beverly Hillbillies, Green Acres, Petticoat Junction, Little House on the Prairie*, and *The Jackie Gleason Show* all portrayed the small farmer and blue-collar worker as a simple, somewhat stupid person, and that image has been the biggest problem for small farmers and ranchers to overcome even today. The parental generation of the sixties and seventies—even my parents—were pushing us kids to go to college and become bankers, doctors, or lawyers. When I was in school in the 1960s and '70s, everyone wanted to be a white-collar worker who made a lot of money, drove the nice car, smoked a cigar, and had the big house in the city. While the blue-collar farmer, logger, plumber, or construction worker took his lunch pail to work every day like Ralph Kramden, in overalls, coming home from work exhausted, broke, and in a sweaty wifebeater, yelling at his wife and kids. Gee, which lifestyle do I want? My folks pushed us to get an education. "Get that degree and you'll have it made; you won't have to work as hard as us parents had to." And girls were always encouraged to "marry a doctor or a lawyer, a banker—that's the better life."

We all strive to make things better for our kids, so their lives will be better than ours. But have we done a disservice over the last three or four generations? Do the kids of tomorrow have a better life than we had? I'm beginning to doubt it. Dad would say, "Go get an education, or else you're going to pull weeds the rest of your life." Well, guess what? I had that white-collar job, with the nice car and big house in the city, and, folks, I didn't like it. Give me the overalls, the pickup truck, and the weeds to pull. A better way of life, in my opinion, is why I farm: to be outdoors in the fresh mountain air, put in a good day of hard work and get some exercise, and reap the harvest of my labor to feed my neighbors.

Today the media and Western society have given young kids expectations beyond reality. Over the last several years reality shows like *American Idol, Iron Chef,* and Donald Trump's *Celebrity Apprentice* ("You're fired!") have brainwashed them to think that if you're not a rock star or instant millionaire, you're nothing. Look at the millions of people that watch these garbage shows and actually believe that's what life is all about. Kids think, "If I don't win *American Idol* I am a failure, a loser." I might actually have to get a REAL JOB. (Heaven forbid that I actually have to work for a living.)

The media and Western society has influenced not only the decline of the small farmer but also the evolution of electronic technology. With Apple breaking into the computer market in the 1970s and the explosion of dot-commers in the 1980s, the direction of the workforce in the United States was transformed. As the computer and electronic age grew in the 1990s and into the twenty-first century, families were more sedentary, split, and further removed from the farms and their backyard gardens than ever before. For those of you in the eighteen- to twenty-five-year-old bracket, think back to the last family relative who was actually a farmer. Probably not very many of you can remember one in the family. Most young people in that age group might have to go back three generations to find a farmer in their family tree. As I attend and work farmers' markets and talk to my customers there, it's almost scary how many kids under sixteen years old have never worked on a farm or even in a garden. Most have no idea where their food comes from, or who grows it. We, as farmers, have a lot of work to do to turn this around. We need to start with the elementary school kids and reintroduce them to fruits and vegetables, and get their hands dirty at an early age. We have to get our kids off the keyboards and back into the earth!

Over the last ten years we have seen a resurgence of young apprentice farmers eager to learn and reverse this trend, but they have some monumental factors facing them, like the high cost of land, lack of available financing, challenging markets, and inexperience. These factors must be addressed by Western society to create a positive environment for new inspired farmers, or the decline will be greater than ever before. Once the old farmers are gone, so is their knowledge and wisdom.

Who will follow? Will only Walmart, WinCo, and Safeway supply us with food from the corporate world?

Chapter 6
SET UP TO FAIL

To forget how to dig the earth and to tend
the soil is to forget ourselves.

~Mahatma Gandhi

Our system sets up the small farmer to fail. What I mean by "system" is the mechanisms currently in place that affect the small farmers' everyday lives. Basically, it's the structure we deal with at the federal, state, and local levels—the emphasis on the financial and tax system, the food system, and the rules and regulatory system. This chapter is a tough one to be positive about because there are true obstacles in place that constrict small farmers to the point that they either can't get started or they fail in the first three years. I will call out vital points that are causing the loss of thousands of family farms annually across America—unless we make major changes in these areas, it is going to be difficult to attract new farmers and try to keep the ones we have.

When you talk to educators and politicians, the buzzwords they often use are "buy local" and "promote and recruit small farmers." It sounds great! Yeah . . . just go out, buy a piece of land, put on some overalls and a straw hat, grow some crops, and we have more small farmers! It's not that easy. To start, how do you become a farmer if you have never had exposure to a farm? Most people today interested in agriculture start by getting some sort of formal education on farming or gardening through community classes or master gardener programs, or they enroll in agriculture curriculums at community colleges and universities. From there, they pursue hands-on experience by way of internships, mentorships, and just plain working on farms to build a knowledge base of the crops they are interested in. Then, most people venture out on their own and begin to look for affordable land or existing farms that are for sale. Under today's financial, tax, food distribution, and regulatory systems there are many unforeseen obstacles that make it very difficult for new farmers to get started, and even more difficult to sustain their farms for the future.

Money Matters: The Financial and Tax System

Let me set up a scenario for you that is typical of what many fellow small farmers and I have had to go through in starting up a small farm. First, let's take our country's financial and tax system. Let's say an apprentice farmer wants to go off on his own and start a small farm. He wants to buy ten acres and grow organic vegetables. He finds ten acres of prime agricultural land with a good well water source. It's listed at $60,000 in a good location close to town. Over the last four years he's been an apprentice on a farm for room and board, earning $500 a month, and his new wife has been on and off unemployment compensation for six months due to the rough economy, but now she has a full-time job flipping burgers at Wendy's for minimum wage. He goes into a lending institution like Wells Fargo or Bank of America, and they give him a great song and dance about how it's no problem to get a loan. Excited, he takes the application home, and he and his wife fill it out and return it the next day. He tells the loan officer that he can put 10 percent down and wants to finance the rest. He submits his wife's W-2 and his Schedule F (a tax form for farming income) from the last year. The loan officer looks it over, and here comes the red flag. "Whoa, we have a problem here; we can accept your wife's W-2 from Wendy's, but we had better leave off your Schedule F because that is a liability that will go against your income."

Farming income is considered "high risk," and your gross income is actually deducted from your net amount; in other words, it puts you in the red. Most institutions will not finance small family farms. That's right, a minimum-wage W-2 from Wendy's makes it easier to finance a piece of property than if your gross farm income is $100,000, but you only net $12,000. The financial system is set up for small farmers to fail. To me, Schedule F means you're fucked, because it puts up the red flag that you are a high risk and nobody will finance you. It sucks, but that's the truth. *To make it easier to farm, the financial system in America needs to consider a farmer's gross earnings, not net earnings.* Everything is deductible on a farm, and the farmer manages the expenses, so lenders should consider gross earnings just like they do for a W-2 pay stub.

So let's continue on with this young couple. They leave all discouraged, and a friend of theirs calls and says, "Hey, I know there are starter programs to help finance beginning farmers. How about Farm Service Agency (FSA)?" FSA is a federal loan program that has loans from 2 to 4 percent. Great! Upon contacting FSA, the agent tells them first that in order to be considered they have to be turned down by at least three lending institutions (which ruins any chances of getting operating credit from lenders), and you must submit a full crop budget projecting the exact amount that you will be making off of the property (which you have no clue what this land could provide because you haven't grown on it before, and it takes three years for you to become organically certified on a new piece of property). So the young couple says, "Ugh . . . that's not going to work." Another financial system set up for small farmers to fail.

Finally, they go to a local sustainable agriculture workshop, and there is a young gal there from California FarmLink, a nonprofit organization that usually is funded by state grants to connect beginning farmers with mentors (older, experienced farmers) or provide them with start-up funds to begin farming. The young couple says, "Great! That's exactly what we've been looking for!" They meet with the young gal and set up the paperwork. They make a business plan that totals $135,000, which includes $54,000 for the land; another $66,000 for the buildings and infrastructure; $10,000 for operating expenses, like seeds, starts, and fertilizers; and $5,000 for marketing, which includes things like community-supported agriculture (CSA) participation, farmers' markets, and packaging.

They sign all the papers, and everyone is happy. The beginning farmer gets his farm, and California FarmLink looks good because they gave the financing to the farmer and now can say, "We have put another small farmer in business." But for how long? Let's face reality: Have they also set them up to fail?

In general, a ten-acre organic vegetable farm can probably gross about $50,000 a year in its first three years for the beginning farmer and his wife. After three years in operation, this young couple has been grossing about $55,000, and their net annual income is about $15,000. They realize that they need to diversify their operation to make more money to sustain the farm. Some of their soils are not great for vegetables so they research other crops that may work better in those soils. At their farmers' market there is a need for blueberries, and after a soil test they decide that's the crop for them. Here we go again! So they say, "Hey, let's go see that gal at California FarmLink; she can help us." They do a business plan and realize that they need $40,000 to buy blueberry plants, trellises, netting, irrigation, boxes, and baskets. They call California FarmLink, and the gal says, "Hey I'm sorry but we only fund new beginning farmers. You're on your own now. Why don't you go Wells Fargo or Bank of America?" Now, the young couple is basically screwed again. On top of that, the young farmer's wife quit her job at Wendy's to help her husband on the farm, so now they don't even have the W-2 to go back to the lending institutions with for security. They're TOAST! The beginning farmer program has left them high and dry. There is no place to go to expand their operation. Creative financing or borrowing from family and friends, building your debt by using up all the credit on your credit cards, or robbing Peter to pay Paul are sometimes the only way to continue financing any expansions of small farms. This now puts the young couple in jeopardy of losing their farm.

The problem most small farmers have is that they are unable to secure more capital to expand their operations, and we must make financing readily available in order to make farming a sustainable and viable option for people. The financial system is broken, and start-up farmer programs set up small farmers to fail. Every farm needs future funding to adjust its operations, and there are no financial avenues for small farmers other than high-interest credit cards or creative financing. This is the real-life situation, and if we want to attract new farmers we had better make it more attractive than the systems we have in place now. There are no financial incentives for small farmers.

In these hard economic times, small farms need access to finances at low interest rates to adapt their farms to additional crops, diversify their markets, establish value-added products (such as jams, jellies, and canned goods), or create venues on the farm for agritourism and ecotourism events. Most small farmers can make a decent living covering their operating costs, but it's very hard to stash money away to cover capital improvements, or to expand their operation without additional financing. There are no tax breaks for farmers other than deductions, and deductions are limited for many because you have to show a profit to get financing. It's a catch-22: you want to deduct as much as possible so you don't pay income tax, but you need to show income to get a loan or financial credit to expand. The tax system leaves you high and dry.

As far as property taxes go, most small farms today are on fewer than one hundred acres. On the federal register, small farms are considered fewer than two hundred acres. Well, sixty years ago more than 10 percent of the American public farmed; today less than 1 percent are farmers. The Williamson Act was established in the early 1960s to preserve land and reduce property taxes for farmers. Currently, if a farmer owns one hundred acres or more, he or she could sign a contract for ten or twenty years with the county and pay only 20 to 75 percent of the property tax. (Check with your county; in Plumas County, farms over eighty acres are eligible.) Many farmers are still benefiting from the Williamson Act. The problem is that most small farmers today own less than one hundred acres and are not eligible to join. My Sierra Valley Farms is a case in point. We own sixty-five acres and have to pay "city-like" property taxes. *Counties today need to reduce acreages in the Williamson contracts down to twenty acres to make the act realistic for most small farmers.*

The tax problems continue until you die, even after death. You work all your life to sustain the family farm and you want to leave it for your children, but if you don't start early and set up a living trust your kids are going to get screwed. Families are hit hard with an estate tax that they can't pay, and often have to sell the property to pay for the probate taxes. Once again, we see that the tax system is set up for small farmers to fail. *We need to eliminate estate taxes on farms, because through them the federal government is contributing to the loss of family farms.*

As far as subsidies, there are none for small farmers. Conglomerates in the commodities of rice, cotton, corn, wheat, and soybeans are the beneficiaries of billions of subsidy dollars annually from the Farm Bill, subsidized by the USDA to grow, or not grow, these crops, depending on global demand. Large companies like Cargill and General Mills influence the global food markets' demands and the prices. The subsidies they receive from the federal government are based on the world price, and supply and demand, of each commodity. The Farm Bill is the bible for this large monoculture of factory farms. All other commodities, such as fruits and vegetables, are considered "specialty crops" in the Farm Bill, and even though California supplies around 50 percent of the United States and much of the world in fruits and vegetables, there are no subsidies for these specialty crops, no matter how large (or small) the companies are.

To small farmers, the Farm Bill is a joke. The government makes a big deal about it every eight years when it is renewed, but it is set up to help the major industrial food and farm corporations producing cotton, corn, wheat, rice, and soybeans and to provide food stamps for the United States. The USDA throws us small farmers a few pennies, mostly for research grants or conservation programs, but nothing that directly helps our pocketbooks. Trust me, nothing free to the small farmer comes from these programs. Usually it's a lot of paperwork, for not much return, and it's done so the bureaucrats look good.

The spokesman for the Farm Bill is the American Farm Bureau Federation (AFBF), commonly referred to as the Farm Bureau, which is supposed to represent and defend the small farmer. As far as I'm concerned, the Farm Bureau is just a front for "big ag." The Farm Bureau is a huge conglomerate financed by large insurance companies and special interests in the biotech industry like Cargill, General Mills, Monsanto, Dow Chemical, and Seneca Foods Corporation. These companies pour millions of dollars into the Farm Bureau to help lobby their special interests in FDA and USDA legislation and regulations, and to get what they want in the Farm Bill. Farm Bureau chapters are set up around the country, usually by counties, and have local, volunteer-elected officials that are just puppets for the big picture. If you read these chapters' bylaws, it's obvious they're backed by right-wing Republicans, who promote big business, factory and industrial farms, the biotech industry, and are proponents for GMO crops. Farm Bureau chapters do very little for small farmers other than to promote them in their newsletter *Ag Alert*, but only if the owner of the small farm is a member. They will throw in an article on organic farming once in a while to look good.

As you can see, I'm not a fan of the Farm Bureau, and I'll tell you why: it's because of a personal experience that happened to me on our farm. In the mid-1990s, we had just set up our organic farm here in Beckwourth, and across the road was a rock quarry that had been selling gravel for years. Not a problem. I can live with that. As the demand for gravel grew, the quarry wanted to expand its opportunities into an asphalt batch plant for the region. Sierra Valley Farms is downwind, and all of its drainage runs across our certified organic property and into the wild and scenic Middle Fork Feather River. Asphalt contains large amounts of oils and arsenic that would have ruined our soils and our organic farm, not to mention all the pollution it would have deposited into the Feather River, a major tributary to the Sacramento Valley and Delta systems. This became a battle, because Plumas County and the quarry were in favor of the asphalt batch plant and we were not. At the time, I was a member of the Plumas-Sierra County Farm Bureau chapter and went to them to help save our farm from the asphalt plant. I thought it was a no-brainer—of course the Farm Bureau would support an organic farmer over an asphalt plant. WRONG! They sided with the asphalt plant because "mining was an accepted practice for the Farm Bureau." Since then I've quit the Farm Bureau and have no use for them. They left us high and dry, and we had to fight the battle ourselves. Thank God for a generous local attorney who represented us for free, and sued Plumas County for not filing an environmental impact report—the asphalt plant was denied and could never be put in place. Hooray for the little guy!

In general, small farmers don't have a "big brother" to help us or speak for our causes. The Farm Bureau is just another spoke in our broken wheel.

Foxes Guarding Henhouses: The Food System

As farmers, our ultimate goal is to provide our customers with the freshest, best-quality food possible. To do so, we must navigate our country's food system, one that's unfortunately clogged up with red tape's muck and mire. Small farmers deal with this food system in many different ways. First and foremost, we try to get our goods to the consumer, which through America's food distribution system is basically done "directly" or "indirectly."

Let's start out with the obvious: selling directly to the consumer. Thousands of years ago our ancestral farmers grew their own food and fed it *directly* to their families and other tribal families. As times changed, fewer farmers grew for their families, and larger farmers grew for many families and delivered to other towns and villages. This later became the food distribution system that we have today, whereby we have a middleman (broker) who coordinates the trucking and shipping of produce worldwide.

Today our food primarily comes to us in this way—*indirectly* from other parts of the country and the world. You basically can get any fruit or vegetable anytime of the year. The four seasons (winter, spring, summer, fall) are not a factor for Walmart, WinCo, Safeway, and other food chains because today the average piece of produce travels about 1,500 miles to your table. That's why it tastes like a rubber ball and looks like one too. Let's follow this journey, say a head of lettuce from California's Salinas Valley traveling to a natural food cooperative store in Salt Lake City, Utah. The head of lettuce is picked by a migrant worker at eight in the morning; it is placed in a basket, then dumped on a conveyer belt, field packed, trucked to a packing shed where it is washed, graded, packed by weight and quantity in a commercial box, labeled, and sent to a cooling facility. From the cooling facility it is bought by a produce broker, a buyer, then travels in a refrigerated truck to a central distributing warehouse center somewhere between San Francisco and Salt Lake City. Sometime in the next two to three days it is bought by a local distributor around Salt Lake City and trucked to this facility and reinventoried. From there, small produce companies purchase that head of lettuce, and it is trucked to the natural food cooperative store and placed in its walk-in cooler until the produce manager and staff place it in the display cooler for the customer to buy. In all, that head of lettuce has taken between four and seven days to end up on that display case. It's then selected by the consumer, checked out by the food clerk, and bagged by the bagger who says, "May I help you out to your car today?" This is pretty normal for most produce, and the fruit coming from outside the country like Mexico and South America travel even farther, picked weeks before you receive it from cold storage.

That's a lot of traveling and handling for one head of lettuce. It's no wonder it lasts only a couple days in the fridge! The USDA estimates that the farmer receives less than seventeen cents out of every dollar spent on produce, and the rest goes to trucking, wholesale distributing, marketing, and retail sales. There is something wrong with the food distribution system in America!

That's why small farmers sell directly to the consumer—we don't want to go through all that and the big distributors don't want to deal with us. Thank God! In reality, the small farmer's only avenue to the general public is usually by direct sales at farmers' markets, roadside stands, U-picks; through CSA box distribution; and by selling to restaurants, co-op stores, and natural food stores. CSAs are basically "subscription farming." A person subscribes to a farm or a series of farms for a set price and period of time, and in return receives a weekly box of food. This concept began in Japan during the 1970s as a way for the consumer to pay the farmer up front for seeds, planting, and harvesting of crops. The consumer would then receive weekly baskets of food throughout the season. Most CSAs are fifteen to twenty weeks long at a cost of fifteen to thirty-five dollars per week, and some offer the option of adding eggs or meat to your weekly vegetable order.

This is America's food distribution system: (1) big food chains and mass distribution, and (2) the small farmer selling direct to the consumer. That's it. There is nothing in between. Based on my estimates, only 5 percent of Californians actually get fresh produce from farmers' markets or from a CSA program, and the other 95 percent buy their produce from the large chains like Safeway, WinCo, and Walmart. *Small farmers need more access to the public, and the public needs more access to the local small farmers.* Small regional food distributors or "hubs" are desperately needed so we can get more of our fresh fruits and vegetables, meats, eggs, milk, cheese, crafts, and value-added products to the consumer. A hub works in this way: small farmers drop off produce to a local food cooperative store (acting as a hub), and the store distributes it to restaurants, schools, and other institutions. They basically become brokers for farmers, helping them sell their products. (I talk more about this in my solutions chapter.)

In addition to the problem of distributing food, there's the problem of labeling what's in it. There is a major disconnect between the USDA and the large corporate factory farms not telling the American public about what's in their food. Just look at the label: there are nutritional facts, but what about all the chemicals and pesticides that have been applied to your fruits, vegetables, and processed foods? Do you, the consumer, actually know what you're eating? How could you? It's not on the label. Oh yeah, they made a big deal about labeling all those so-called nutrients, so you can see how fat you're going to get, but isn't it more important to know if your apple's been sprayed with a carcinogen?

About fifteen years ago when I went back to farming, the organic movement was just getting into full swing. With my farm situated at the headwaters of the Middle Fork Feather River, I wanted to be the best steward of the land that I could and certify my land as organic so that I could minimize my footprint in Sierra Valley. Boy, did I have a rude awakening! Not only does the food system make the organic farmer jump through a tangle of hoops, but you also have to pay through the nose. The USDA's National Organic Program (NOP) was set up to provide national organic standards for small farmers to follow in order to become certified organic. A farmer must adhere to these standards and jump through these hoops to become certified organic (visit ccof.org for all the details). I'll summarize them here for you. First, you must apply to a third-party organic certifier (a neutral inspector), and the main three are California Certified Organic Farmers (CCOF), Quality Assurance International (QAI), and Oregon Tilth. (Many states have their own certifiers. Check with your local and state offices.) Each certifier will require you to:

1. Submit an application and pay a per-acre fee for membership, and a fee to be inspected annually.

2. Submit an affidavit from the agricultural commissioner that no pesticides or conventional fertilizers have been applied on the property for the past three years. If so, there will be a three-year quarantine, or transitional period.

3. Complete an Organic System Plan (OSP) that is your bible, a complete detail of the farm, fields, crops, and how they will be grown and managed and what inputs (fertilizers and amendments, for example) you will be using, how they will be handled and labeled, and where products will be sold and housed.

4. Register with the state, pay a fee, and submit certification.

5. Once successful, there are annual fees for all of the above.

Basically, small organic farmers have to sign their lives away and pay through the nose to verify they haven't used any chemicals or pesticides. The irony is that the big corporate factory, industrial, and conventional farms are not required to tell the consumer about any chemicals or pesticides they have used on your fruits and vegetables. The organic industry got a lobotomy on this one! Basically organic farmers pay to use nothing, while the "villains" get off scot-free and can spray anything they want and not have to tell you about it. That's the American way!

Consumers, wake up! Demand these conventional farms put everything they use on the label. You have to help save the organic farmer, so we can continue to sell you fresh, safe food. *The consumer must put the pressure on our legislators and demand that every chemical, fertilizer, pesticide, and GMO crop be on that label.* We need to protect our food system, and know what we are putting in our bodies, in order for us to live healthy, productive lives. It's disgusting what industrial and factory farms apply to our fruits, vegetables, dairy, and meat products. As of today, conventional farms are not required to put anything on the labels. They are only required to meet "pesticide residual levels," and you don't even know what they are, and neither do I. The FDA and USDA are full of ex-industrial, biotech, and factory farm representatives that protect their interests.

The fox is guarding the henhouse! This must change. In 2012, a petition circulated in California and received enough signatures to put Proposition 37 on the ballot to require that all GMO ingredients in our foods be placed on food labels; since the USDA would not require it, the public spoke out. After a dirty campaign by the pro-GMO conglomerates like Dow, Monsanto, and the Farm Bureau, the proposition was defeated, and as of today GMOs are not listed on our food labels anywhere.

Apples and Oranges: The Rules and Regulatory System

The last and most frustrating of systems for small farmers is the maze of federal, state, and local rules and regulations, as well as the land use and zoning regulations that only allow farmers to operate a certain way in a certain area. There are fees for EVERYTHING! From agricultural licenses to producer certificates, state and federal organic fees, certifier fees, USDA and CDFA fees—FEES, FEES, FEES. These extra costs nitpick farmers to their deathbeds, and these are the little ones. What has contributed most to the death of the small farmer over the last forty years are the major rules and regulations that our legislators and congresspeople have put in place. Over the years, the large corporate farms have reversed these onto the small farmer to put them out of business, while they lobby governmental officials to be more lenient on the true offenders, the factory farms. Rules and regulations are going to continue to squeeze the little guy out. It must be stopped. *We must hammer our local legislators to develop local laws and regulations that supersede these federal and state laws to reduce constricting regulations on the small farmers.*

Among the strongest regulations on farmers are those for the dairy and beef industry. As the small dairy and cattle operations were going out of business, the larger farms, especially the feed lots (used to fatten up cows before slaughter), could not handle the waste problems that came with more animals, and the regulators stepped in to set rules to combat this problem. To compound this issue, cows were ingesting so much corn—their stomachs were not designed to break down all the *Escherichia coli* (*E. coli*) bacteria created by corn—and serious outbreaks occurred that caused the USDA to set even stronger regulations for all farmers big and small.

Forty years ago we never had *E. coli* problems in our produce, meat, or dairy products, because we never fed corn to our cows. Corn is the source of the problem for *E. coli* bacteria. Cows were never meant to eat corn; they are pasture grass animals. Michael Pollan describes in detail in his book *The Omnivore's Dilemma* that the cow's digestive system is not able to properly digest corn to eliminate *E. coli* bacteria. Today, huge factory farms house hundreds of cows in feedlots, feed them heavy amounts of corn, and inject numerous hormones and vaccinations to fight disease and to build up their weight before slaughter. The *E. coli* bacteria is then passed on in the milk and the meat tissue. European studies have shown that grass-fed cows have no source of *E. coli* bacteria, and that six to eight weeks of "finishing" (final feeding period before slaughter) cows out to pasture in grass can eliminate the *E. coli* bacteria.

For small farmers, waste and corn are not issues because they don't keep large quantities of animals in a confined area, and their cows are put out to pasture, not intensively fattened with corn. The problem is that the small farmers still must comply with the regulations of the large factory farms, causing them to invest large amounts of money into waste-treatment measures and pay absurd amounts of money in fees for *E. coli* testing and sampling that is not needed. These strong regulations have also caused processing plants to go out of business, and make very few available to small farmers.

In addition, large corporations like McDonald's monopolize the big beef industry to dictate the meat markets and the price, and lobby to reduce the number of USDA processing plants and inspectors to reduce competition. If there are no small processing plants or inspectors, small meat producers cannot get their meats processed or inspected. The plants that are available are so impacted and few and far between that small meat producers can't get in, or cannot make ends meet because of the travel costs of transporting live animals long distances to these plants. USDA has contributed to eliminating the small meat farmer (beef, lamb, pork, poultry, etc.) not only by reducing the number of processing plants and inspectors but also by enacting rules and regulations for on-farm processing that are so ridiculous that small meat producers can't survive. For example, you can buy a lamb from a farmer who can kill it and process it right in front of you, and you can take it home, but the farmer cannot kill it, process it, and take it to a farmers' market and sell it—that has to go to a USDA-inspected processing plant. What's the difference? Why not train college kids to work as inspectors and have them on-site? Problem solved.

The dairy industry follows the same model. Over the years, a few large dairy factory farms have lobbied our legislators to believe that the small dairy farmer must follow the same rules and regulations that they follow. The only reason I can see for them to do this is to put the small dairies out of business. There is no reason that small independent dairies would generate nearly the amount of animal waste as the large factory farms.

Yet the USDA has imposed the same large-waste requirements on the small dairy farmers as required for the factory farms. As I explained earlier, factory farm dairies emit large amounts of animal waste in small areas that pollute our waterways and air quality. Huge methane "eaters" are now being used to try and remove the urea waste and reduce the air and nitrate pollution going into the environment. The USDA, pushed by the conglomerate factory dairies, has imposed these same regulations on the small dairy farmers, and it's putting them out of business because they are expected to put in the same amount of equipment and waste facilities, and they simply can't afford it. We're comparing apples and oranges here, but money talks and bullshit walks and corporate America wins again.

When I was a kid, my uncles milked cows twice a day. They would separate the cream and the milk, and the skim would go with the grain to make slop to feed the pigs. We drank the milk right out of the cow, and then it was filtered and went into the refrigerator. No one ever got sick. The problem today is fear. The large dairies and regulators have built fear into the public that raw milk is bad. It's nothing new, folks! It's the way things were done before these idiots took over. When you pasteurize anything, you kill everything! Years ago our immune systems were accustomed to the bacteria in things like cow's milk, goat milk, and raw cheese because it was in our common diet. We had it all as kids: raw milk and cream, homemade cottage cheese, yogurt, mascarpone, ricotta cheese, and fresh and cured meats like beef, pork, lamb, goat, deer, waterfowl, and upland game. Nobody got sick because our immune systems were used to the common bacteria that are in unpasteurized products. On top of that, the meat was brown, because it was aged, not dyed red and pumped with hormones so it looks "pretty." The old-timers would slaughter and then age the meat in a cool root cellar or a cool, aerated barn for a week or so to help break down the fibers in the meat tissue, making it more tender. The meat would have a brownish color to it; that's normal! In processing plants today, they don't have time to age the meat because the American public gets irate when it has to wait in line at the McDonald's drive-thru for that quarter-pound cheeseburger. To save time, the meat giants just pump up that cow with corn and hormones so they don't have to age its meat, and McDonald's cooks the shit out of it to get rid of the *E. coli* bacteria. "Here's your order, sir . . . " What a great country we live in!

People, wake up! We need to stop these USDA corporate regulators from strangling the small farmer. Do away with these corporate rules and regulations on small farms and ranches but keep them where they're needed, on factory farms. We need to go back to the old days when you bought your food from the local butcher, baker, farmer, and milkman who delivered the milk fresh (that's why he had to deliver it, because it wasn't pasteurized and would spoil if not refrigerated) to your door. You knew where your fruits, vegetables, meats, and dairy products were grown and raised—in your community—and who raised it. Like the small farmer said to the McDonald's executive, "You can't beat my meat." No, they can't! *Our systems are set up for the small dairy and beef farmers to fail, and we must fix them by removing these ridiculous regulations on small farmers and ranchers and allow them to sell direct to the consumer.* I will go into more detail in my solutions chapter.

Chapter 7
DIVERSIFY, DIVERSIFY, DIVERSIFY

When tillage begins, other arts follow;
farmers, therefore, are the founders of
human civilization.

~Daniel Webster

It had been a few years now that I had been self-employed. No more sucking off the tit of the taxpayers. No company car. No health insurance. No retirement. No benefits. No company parties or paid seminars. Farming was just plain hard work! Just as I remembered it when I was a kid. The major difference was that I felt good coming in at night all dusty and dead tired from a good day's work. I still to this day grab a glass of wine or cocktail and take a stroll at sunset to look at my labors of the day. I say to myself, "Man, I get to live, work, and play in God's country . . . it doesn't get any better than this!" The problem is that I have to make a living in God's country.

It was becoming apparent to me that Sierra Valley was a crazy place to be farming. Of all the places in California to save a family farm, why did it have to be in one of the harshest places on Earth to grow anything? Why couldn't it have been in the lush Sacramento Valley or on the beautiful California coast? No, it had to be an alpine valley of extremes, here in Beckwourth, California, nestled in the northwest corner of Sierra Valley. We have only forty to sixty frost-free days a year for our growing season, and many years we have frost every month. Our summer daily temperatures can fluctuate from fifty to sixty degrees during the day, with mornings a chilly thirty degrees and afternoons hitting a dry heat of over ninety degrees. Sierra Valley, being the highest alpine valley in the Western Hemisphere, spanning over two hundred square miles, is a lot like Lake Tahoe: it creates its own weather patterns. Sierra Valley winters are a "wonderland," with the frozen tundra receiving as much as twenty feet of snow throughout the season; temperatures may drop to twenty below zero at night, and may not reach much above zero in the daytime for weeks in December and January. Sierra Valley winters are full of migrating waterfowl, with over-wintering hawks and eagles on every fence post. The winter winds drift any amount of snow sideways, piling it up at every doorway. We get a workout, spending hours each day plowing, shoveling, and replowing and reshoveling the driveway and doorways. In spring, we begin to thaw out, and up come the lush meadow grasses with Sierra Valley full of breeding birds and wildflowers. Despite its beauty, it's a frustrating place to farm because you spend most of the day with your face down in the dirt, trying to plant seeds and transplants, pulling weeds, harvesting crops, or laying down drip irrigation lines while that Sierra Valley wind sends your hat flying, and the heat and dust make you look like a coal miner at the end of the day. Due to the morning cold and the wind, along with the afternoon heat, you're constantly putting on and taking off layers of clothing throughout the day.

I finally came to realize that Sierra Valley is a land of diversity, in climate, geology, and animal and plant life. So why fight it? I should farm with it. Go with the flow! Our growing season is so short that in the early years between 1998 and 2004 we realized that we could not make a living only on crops that grew from June through September. We had to diversify our operation. Luckily, I was able to secure our mortgage, our operating line of credit, and our equity lines while I still had the W-2 from my parks and recreation job, but by 2004, finances were beginning to dwindle because we were not able to make enough money off of the vegetable and native plant operations. Our farm was becoming a money pit. Improvements and repairs were eating up our annual income and equity lines—projects like redrilling failed wells, replacing well pumps and boilers, installing energy efficient equipment, retrofitting buildings for energy efficiency by replacing windows and siding, adding efficient appliances, and converting to a geoexchange heating system for the greenhouse to replace inefficient propane heaters. It was also time to upgrade our obsolete equipment to reduce labor and repair costs that were killing us, so we purchased newer tractors, a potting machine for the nursery, and labor-saving tractor implements. It was all putting us in the red. We had no savings left, our credit cards and home equity lines were maxed out, and we had to get creative, borrowing from friends and my folks. I had to find a way to survive and get through this crisis. We weren't even talking sustainability; we were in survival mode, Darwin's "survival of the fittest." We needed more pieces to this puzzle. The solution: diversify, diversify, diversify!

Each winter, Kim and I evaluated our operation as to what worked that year and what didn't. Around 2005, we realized that we needed to really diversify our operation to bring in a variety of incomes to make ends meet. Because of our rural community, there were no high-paying full-time or seasonal jobs that we could take on for side income, plus Joey was an infant—we would have needed to pay for day care and it would be a wash anyway. So I decided to add ventures to the farm. I set up the farm as an "annual pie," with each quarter a season, and every slice within that season a month. I then made an overlay of our income based on the same strategy to see where we needed to bring in more income to cover our expenses. The answer: everywhere! It was everywhere! It was clear and to the point that I had better find a way to bring in more income or we might lose the farm. I decided that the only approach was to develop high-dollar crops, more markets, and create venues on the farm. I looked at every facet of our operation to utilize every income avenue possible, and to reduce as much expense as possible. My biggest asset throughout this process was that I wasn't afraid to fail, or maybe I was just a dumb, stubborn Italian, like Nonno Romano. But I was determined to find a solution!

My approach to farming involves the following: research, compare and contrast, make an educated guess, don't put all your eggs in one basket, and if it looks good, go for it! Evaluate its success, but give it time. Don't just try it for a year and if it fails chuck the idea. Build on it. Even if things fail, learn from them and try not to make the same mistakes twice. During my research, I found that there were no high-elevation gardening or farming books available, not even from our UC Extension office. I had to learn how to grow crops in this crazy climate by keeping my own logs and statistics. Studying how crops grow in our soils, climates, seasons, and microclimates is a learning curve that never stops. Over the years, I have found that no two seasons are alike. Why, I don't even know what's "normal" in Sierra Valley. The old-timers say, "All you have in Sierra Valley is July and winter," and I'm starting to believe they are right. It is a crazy place to farm. You definitely can't be a type A personality here—someone who needs to follow a set, routine schedule, and gets stressed when having to venture too far off course—that's for sure! To farm in the Sierra a person needs to be flexible and be able to change course on a moment's notice. So with that in mind, I thought, "Hey, I need to think out of the box to farm in this crazy place," and that's what I did. The next problem was money. "It takes money to make money"—and that was our dilemma; we didn't have the money. It became frustrating for Kim to justify some of the start-up funds we needed to diversify our operation. We began extending ourselves to the point that it stressed our marriage, and we were surpassing our credit lines. We had to figure out how to hang on.

Because we are in rural Plumas County, geographically one of the largest counties in California but with just over twenty thousand people, we realized that we needed to market our produce in a number of different ways. CSA programs (subscription farming) were getting popular at the time, but were not for us because of the wide distribution of our resident population. So farmers' markets and direct sales to restaurants and natural food stores seemed to be the path to continue on. But all these outlets were a good drive from home, ranging from forty to sixty miles away. I really wanted a way to sell directly to our rural community. I kept the old buildings intact here on the farm for nostalgic value, but it was apparent to me that agritourism was becoming popular in California and people wanted to visit old farms because they were increasingly becoming extinct. I had started attending farmers' markets in Truckee, Tahoe City, and Reno and noticed that I was coming home empty after every market, and that I should be bringing back produce for our Plumas County residents. In 1998, there were no farmers' markets within fifty miles of our farm, not even in our whole county or neighboring Sierra County. We had a great old granary by the side of the road that was a prime location to set up a roadside stand. So I said to Kim, "Why don't we turn that old granary into a produce stand? I'll buy produce from the farmers after the farmers' market, and we can sell it at our farm stand." That's what we did. We made a commitment to our community that Sierra Valley Farms will provide the freshest and most local produce available as long as we're in business. Our mission was full customer and community service—just like the old days when a handshake was good enough. It was a hit! We continued to bring in more and more produce, until we couldn't get any more out of the farmers' market growers at a wholesale price.

During the winter of 2007, I said to Kim, "You know we have a mailing list of over three hundred people, and I know all the farmers and chefs. Why not create an on-site farmers' market and bring the farmers to the customer?" After some heavy deliberation, we came to the agreement that that was the best solution, and it paid off. We applied to California Food and Agriculture's (CDFA) Department's farmers' market division and were able to have a certified farmers' market here on the farm. We began soliciting and sole-sourcing farmers for their quality and diversity of product. We wanted limited competition so that each farmer would make money, and we wanted a "one-stop shop," where our customers could get all their major groceries—local meat, wild fish, organic vegetables, dairy products, baked goods, wine, and a variety of fruits, berries, and nuts—plus a wide assortment of value-added products as well as local food vendors and an attraction, such as guest chef cooking demonstrations. Would that be possible in Beckwourth, California, a small town of four hundred people? You bet! Because we made a commitment to our community ten years before and we kept our word. Today we run our market as Romano's Farmers' Market at Sierra Valley Farms, every Friday from the first Friday of June through the third Friday of September from 10 a.m. to 2 p.m. We have become a destination farmers' market, attracting more than four hundred people every Friday to shop, enjoy our free guest chef cooking demonstrations (celebrity chefs from the Reno/Tahoe area), explore scenic Plumas/Sierra County, and visit the quaint shops in our towns of Portola and Graeagle. To this day, we are the only certified on-farm farmers' market in California, and creating this on-farm farmers' market has not only brought fresh, local produce, meats, and dairy products to the community, but by bringing together chefs, farmers, crafters, and local residents it has become a gathering place for the community to come and socialize for hours.

The concept has been so successful that we have developed a model for other rural communities to follow (see Appendix A). This agritourism thing was a good fit for us because we had the right formula. We were well known and the only game in town. Plus, we were an old family, in Sierra Valley since 1907, and the buildings are testament to that! People could come to the farm and see where their food comes from, plus have a glass of wine (or two) with the farmer who grew it! We took this phenomenon a step further in 2008 when I got a call from my favorite chef, Mark Estee of Moody's Bistro in Truckee. Mark wanted to host a benefit dinner on the farm for Project Mana, a local food bank. He asked, "Do you have a venue where we can put on a dinner for about fifty people?" I had just the spot—an old barn that my uncle Emilio built in

Romano's Farmers' Market, photo courtesy of Roger Freeburg

"Dinners in the Barn" are held inside this barn, built in 1938.

1938. We packed it with equipment in the winter, but it sat vacant all summer. "It's nothing fancy," I said. "But it doesn't leak!" So we set up a temporary kitchen area, got the Plumas County permits, and Mark and Moody's catering chefs put on the benefit dinner, which was a huge success. We continued to diversify our operation the following year when Mark and I got together and created a summer series, "Dinners in the Barn," with Moody's at Sierra Valley Farms. We featured the concept of "from the field to the fork": meet your farmer, meet your chef, and know where your food comes from. For the dinners, which we continue to host, everything is picked fresh that day from the farm, and the Moody's catering chefs locally source all the other ingredients to develop the menu. We feature a four-course gourmet dinner, with a farm tour, a wine purveyor, and a dinner musician. A total sellout! Eight dinners a summer, and the proceeds help Sierra Valley Farms feed the pie. (In 2010, we made the *Sierra Sun*, our local newspaper, and its "Top Ten Things to Do" at Lake Tahoe. Who would have thought all of this in little Beckwourth, California? Anything is possible!)

Small farms today have to be adaptable to change. Nothing is forever. Many times a good venture goes sour because of unforeseeable situations. A case in point was our ecotourism venture, the Waterfowl Hunting Club that I ran for fifteen years. When I moved to the farm in 1990, I was a big hunter and had spent years hunting waterfowl with my uncles here in Sierra Valley. I wanted to continue to hunt and thought that if I created a hunting club, I could continue to finance my hobby. I leased a 1,400 acre ranch in Sierra Valley and solicited friends to join the club. The club was an instant success and became profitable, and a vital part of our winter income. The first ten years (1990–2000) were successful because I would manage the weirs at the dam that my uncles built in the early thirties. This three-hundred-foot small dam had four spillways that my uncles would close and open up to manage the meadows for summer cattle grazing. They would put two-by-six planks in each spillway to limit the amount of water needed to flood the meadows, for feed production, and to recharge aquifers for their shallow, windmill-driven wells.

My uncles were the ultimate stewards of the land. The meadows were lush, not overgrazed, and they used this "flooding" technique to diversify the pastures and grow rye, oats, barley, and winter wheat; to bale hay; and to thrash the grain for their livestock. When I started the hunting club, I would continue their practice by putting the planks into the weirs and flooding the meadows. The cover was lush for spring waterfowl nesting, breeding, and brooding. Come hunting season, the cattle had been pulled from the pastures by Labor Day, and the slough channels were full of feed and eight-foot reed cover. I managed the club so that there were only enough members for the birds to comfortably support. Everyone always got a limit, and there were plenty of waterfowl to continue their life cycle after the season. When the battle came up over the asphalt plant across the road, things changed. The landowner, who owns the weirs, also owns the quarry—you see where this is going, right? Over the next seven years, more cattle was added to the land, and grazing was extended from September to the end of December, which overgrazed the pastures and trampled the slough channels. In addition, upstream water users overdiverted the water for their land to the point that the club had no water for the waterfowl or the cattle, or to maintain the sloughs. The sloughs dried up, and the cattle then ate all the reeds and cover—the waterfowl habitat was gone. I gave up the hunting club in 2004 because it had become a wasteland and couldn't support any waterfowl populations. People today still don't understand where the waterfowl have gone. It's simple: somewhere where there is food, water, and cover—duh! When you are leasing land, you are at the mercy of the landowner. It's out of your control; you just can't predict the future, and all good things come to an end.

These were ventures that helped diversify the operation of the farm, but they weren't freebies. We still had expenses like product and property liability, permits, and licenses, and these ventures only covered short periods of time. Other ventures didn't work so well for us. One was a pumpkin patch that we held for three years. Sierra Valley is too cold to grow pumpkins, so we covered an old broccoli patch with straw and drove down to the Sacramento Valley to get a couple of bins of pumpkins. We put them out in the field a couple weeks before Halloween so that the kids could come out and select their pumpkins. We added activities like face painting, a bouncy house, hayrides, and even pony rides. It worked fine for the first couple of years because we had unusually nice weather, but the following year we got down in the single digits and received a foot of snow. All the pumpkins turned black and rotted. So much for that venture. Sierra Valley weather is just too unpredictable. We considered selling Christmas trees, but who wants to sit outside and sell trees when it's ten below zero? Not to mention, for ten dollars you can get a permit from the Forest Service and cut a beautiful silvertip fir yourself.

Year after year, to this day, we still need to annually evaluate our operation to continue to sustain the farm. We still have slices of pie with no income that we need to fill to live a comfortable life here. Looking back, it seems that every time we got ahead there was an unexpected expense: another pump went out, or a piece of equipment broke, or the lender wasn't going to extend our line of credit. That was the case in 2010, when it was back to "another get-rich-quick scheme by Gary Romano." "Oh no," Kim said, "not another winter of Gary trying to come up with another project that only costs us money. I've yet to see where any of them have done any good—we're still broke, you're in denial, we're always losing money on your ideas!" Maybe she was right, and my ventures were leading to suicide with a butter knife, the slow death of our farm. But that's the only way I know how to farm, to continue to diversify my crops and operation. I was going to go down with the ship and keep farming. We were still paying our bills, and that's all I could ask for at the time. You have to realize that there are not enough markets to sustain a farm in a small rural area on one or two ventures. You need multiple incomes and money coming in every month to offset the annual expenses.

So I continued on my quest as planned, to increase our income and find new crops for Sierra Valley Farms. I had established my annual and perennial field crops: spring mixes, spinach, romaine lettuce, arugula, kale, radishes, Swiss chard, sorrel, carrots, beets, broccoli, broccoli raab, cabbage, green onions, shallots, horseradish, asparagus, and garlic. I would begin in late April when I could turn the ground, and plant only what I could manage myself, with a few volunteers or interns. Basically, I would plant a third of an acre of these crops every ten days, and continue planting until Labor Day. This would give me enough crops to attend four farmers' markets a week and supply a CSA, ten restaurants, and a few natural food stores in the Reno/Tahoe area. It was full-time: seven days a week, 5 a.m. to 9 p.m. every day from the end of April until the ground started to freeze at the end of October. No vacations. Time to make hay when the sun shines! I had a couple of perennial crops to support our annual crops, such as asparagus (May–July) and horseradish (October–March). Our original heated greenhouse had all the tools to propagate our native plants and vegetable transplants, and manage diverse environments for specialty crops like microgreens and wasabi. We had imported wasabi plants from a nursery in the Northwest about eight years earlier and were successfully growing them in the heated greenhouse. Since then, we've made our own wasabi paste and microgreens, both currently available. This is evidence of yet another diversification of our operation: a value-added (processed) food item that we could sell year round. This was a slice missing from our pie. We also found that horseradish did really well in our deep alluvial soils, so we found a small bottler in Reno and got him certified organic, and began an organic line of horseradish and horseradish-mustard condiments under the name of Romano

Organics. We took our horseradish a step further when I had an idea one winter to use our organic horseradish to make a line of organic cocktail mixers—that's what long winters in Sierra Valley do to a farmer, coming up with these crazy ventures! We started with Bloody Mary and Tequila Maria mixes, and since then have added margarita, mai tai, and pomegranate/cranberry mixes for organic martinis and cosmopolitans.

But we still had gaps in our pie. There were slices during the fall, winter, and spring with no income, and somehow I had to find more crops to fill those gaps. I decided to diversify my operation even more by adding hoop houses to try and extend our season. In 2010 we were able to secure Natural Resources Conservation Service (NRCS) funding (33 percent cost share) for a twenty-by-fifty-foot hoop house, and bought another fifteen-by-forty-foot one from a neighbor, and were able to construct them that year.

In addition, I had a unique opportunity in December of 2011 to do a crop-share agreement with a neighbor in an abandoned greenhouse. One of my previous interns and her fiancé had bought a cutting horse ranch that had a massive "sunken" greenhouse, built by the previous owner, but it never got into operation. I called it the "bunker." It is huge, thirty feet by one hundred feet, and dug into the earth seven feet down, with a plexiglass and cantilevered roof and forty-inch perimeter raised beds. It had sat vacant for about fifteen years, so I took it over in January of 2011 and put it into production by March of that year. It was another learning curve on how to grow indoors during the harshest months of the year in Sierra Valley (October–March). In these hoop houses and the "bunker" we experimented with heirloom tomatoes, cucumbers, artichokes, winter greens, specialty melons, snow peas, beans, beets, carrots, broccoli, cabbage, sweet peppers, herbs, and strawberries—all with limited success.

The one thing I do know is that I can grow year round in one of the craziest places to farm on Earth. Despite all these ventures and additional crops, we head into 2013 again with financial uncertainty. One of my dreams here at Sierra Valley Farms is to "go green" and reduce our footprint on the headwaters of the Middle Fork Feather River. With that in mind, we are installing solar to offset 50 percent of our power needs, and we are changing over our diesel tractors to be fueled by biodiesel from a local biodiesel plant right here in Sierra Valley (Simple Fuels Biodiesel) that refines cooking grease and oils from restaurants in the Reno/Tahoe area. Over the next few years we hope to phase our trucks to biodiesel and add wind power to assist our solar system, and as always to diversify, diversify, diversify!

The farm house and front field hoop house, photo courtesy of Roger Freeburg.

Chapter 8

MEET YOUR TWENTY-FIRST CENTURY
SMALL FARMER

Bowed by the weight of centuries he leans
Upon his hoe and gazes on the ground,
The emptiness of ages in his face,
And on his back the burden of the world.
~Edwin Markham
from "The Man with the Hoe"

As I spent more time farming over the last fifteen years and attending so many farmers' markets and struggling to make a living, I thought, "Are all the farmers in the same boat as I am, trying to make a living farming?" As I looked around the farmers' markets, I realized that today most small farmers farm for many different reasons, and that relying solely upon the farm for one's source of income is actually rare. Today, most small farmers farm for an additional source of income or as a hobby. In other words, you better keep your day job because you can't make a living on farming alone.

You know, when Larry and I were kids working the San Francisco Flower Market in our teens, I would look at all the flower growers in the early morning hours and think of them as "just like Dad": they were about the same age, they were family farmers, and flowers were their life's work and their only source of income. The flower market was segregated by ethnicity—like the Italian market, the Japanese market, and the Chinese market—but flowers were everyone's livelihood, as it had been for generations before them. They were old families like ours, from all over the Bay Area. When the flower industry started to unravel in the late 1980s and 1990s, many of those old families began to give up their livelihood. Today, when I go down to the flower market with Dad, I don't know a soul, and neither does he. Only a few of the outside stores are still the same. "You know, all the old-timers are gone," Dad says. "Look at all the flowers from South America; they bring them in so cheap, too many of them, and they can't sell them all. They have to dump them—look at all of them in the dumpster. There are not many florists anymore, only housewives that come in to buy them cheap. Remember all the flowers we use to sell to the wholesale flower shippers? No more!"

So who is the modern-day small farmer? If you ask kids and most of society to draw a farmer, it will be a guy in his forties or fifties, wearing overalls and a wide-brimmed hat, with a straw sticking out of his mouth, holding a pitchfork—that image hasn't changed. If you say draw an organic farmer, drop the age by twenty years, add dreadlocks, and replace the straw in his mouth with a joint. I'm being a little stereotypical here, but that's reality. Through all the changes that have happened to the small farmer, our perception of them has stayed the same. But it's not true in the real world. Today's small farmers are a wide array of ex-professionals, retirees, old and young folks, and everything in between. I've come up with ten classifications, not so much by ethnic origins but instead by sociological classification. They share one common denominator: a passion to farm and/or to live, or to pretend to live "the farming lifestyle." Just go to a farmers' market in your own hometown and take a stroll; it's great farmer watching. There are all types and colors, from different walks of life, who farm for different reasons. There are:

- the ethnic farmers;
- the born-again farmers;
- the hobby farmers;
- the family heritage farmers;
- the organic farmers;
- the big-hat-no-cattle farmers;
- the antiestablishment farmers;

- the got-it-together farmers;
- the wannabe farmers;
- the greenhorn farmers; and
- the rest, which fall into a number of these categories.

To start, consider the ethnic farmers—a classification my Romano family certainly fell under. This group is composed of tight-knit farming families of specific ethnic origins. Mostly Asian farmers (Hmong, Vietnamese, Chinese, Indian, or Japanese), Hispanic or Latino farmers (Mexican, South American, Spanish), European farmers (Italian, German, French), or Middle Eastern farmers (Afghan, Muslim descent), these groups specialize in crops from their homeland and combine families together to mainly rent or lease land to grow these crops or sell their prepared foods. They utilize their extended families (young children, parents, aunts, uncles, and grandparents) to work the fields and attend the markets. There is no hired help in this group.

Then we have the born-again farmer. Like myself, this type was born into farming, went away because he or she didn't want to farm, but later in life realized that it wasn't so bad after all and returned. These farmers have typically done a complete career change, usually leaving a good job behind to go back to the family farm.

Due to the economic woes of the last five years, and people wanting to buy five to ten acres in the country, the hobby farmer has developed. This farmer is usually a middle-aged husband-and-wife team, in which one has a secured job and the other keeps a seasonal or part-time job or is semiretired (e.g., teacher, government job). They grow crops during the summer, or seasonally, to supplement their income. They attend a farmers' market for a period of time, or for a specific crop, like mandarins, apples, peaches, or blueberries. Once the season is done they then go back to their day job, and we won't see them again until the next year. They are usually dedicated to farming that particular season or crop(s), and play a major role at farmers' markets.

The most respected farmer at any farmers' market is the family heritage farmer, the "old-world farmer" who comes from generations of farming. Grandpa is still selling that broccoli with his son and grandson by his side. They have the same old wooden boxes, and that same old truck that they take to market every week, rain or shine. The great-grandfathers paid off the farm, and everything is paid cash, free and clear. It's all that we aspire to be as farmers. These families have been around for generations, and they are not going anywhere.

The most obvious are the die-hard organic farmers. This group lives and breathes organically. They are the stereotypical organic farmer in dreadlocks, wool socks, and Birkenstocks. They farm in the purest sense of the soil, composting and living green. As an organic farmer myself, I farm with these ideals; I just don't look the part. I don't have the hair! These farmers often utilize the Worldwide Opportunities on Organic Farms (WWOOF) program and interns for labor, and are usually the younger generation, under forty years old. They are very creative and earthy.

On the opposite end of the spectrum is the big-hat-no-cattle rancher. This is the farmer that really bothers me. You see this group mostly in the ranching community. These are the people with corporate money from another occupation that go out and decide that they are going into the cattle, hay, or farming business. They like to play the part of the farmer or rancher, but it's really just a write-off for their corporate business. They go out and spend hundreds of thousands of dollars on big tractors, combines, and livestock, but their annual operations don't bring in enough to support the business. It's a front for them; they hire a foreman and ranch managers, and never get their hands dirty. They tend to squeeze the little guy out of the farmers' market because they can spend more money on marketing their product. Farming or ranching is not in their hearts, nor in their best interest.

A new group that is gaining ground is the antiestablishment farmer. This is the young, corporate employee that is "just a number" in the business world—stifled by corporate America, with no recognition, sitting in a cubicle going nowhere, with no job security. Clueless as to what farming is all about, he or she doesn't really care. They strive for the freedom of being their own boss; they believe that they are more secure in farming than the alternative, no matter what the crops are. They are looking to farming to increase their assets, and as a great opportunity to live healthier, happier lives. This will be an interesting group to watch in the future.

The next group, the got-it-together farmers, is where I've always wanted to be. They are the trendsetters and visionaries in the small farm industry. Examples in my Northern California region are Full Belly Farm, Happy Girl Farms, Niman Ranch, Capay Organic, and many others. They have been the innovators and leaders in organics, saving heirloom seeds, fighting GMO crops, and inspiring us all to do what we do. They have set the industry standards for healthy, high-quality organic foods, and are the best stewards of the land, striving for excellence. I can't put my finger on why this group has been so successful other than they have the "it" factor—they just have put all the pieces of the puzzle in the right places.

There is always the one bad apple that spoils the box. It's the wannabe farmer. This is the retiree, or "ex-car salesman," that goes into farming or selling a value-added product thinking that he or she is going to make a killing. They have a big retirement pension, are fat and out of shape, and bring their corporate values to the farmers' market. All they care about is: "How much did you make today?" They just do farmers' markets and know very little about the product or how to grow it. They hire out the farm because all they want to do is make money. They disrespect what the small farmer's values are all about. These people usually last a couple of years and go out of business. Who in their right mind would want to go into farming for the money?

The last group of farmers is the one that I am most worried about—the greenhorn farmers. This group probably has the biggest passion to get into farming. They are young, often in their twenties, and are book-smart farmers that know all the terms and fancy words, but have never worked a day in their life on a farm. Or if they have, they lack the natural instinct to farm, that is, they weren't born and bred working the land. This group is scary to me because they are our future farmers. They are going to have to grow food for my children and my children's children. The odds are stacking higher against them as land gets more expensive, financing is harder to get, marketing and food distribution become major obstacles, and the bottom line is that farming is *always* hard work. This group needs mentors like myself, and older farmers, to teach them farming skills and the ropes of becoming successful farmers, because many of them don't even know which end of the shovel to hold. Literally. They lack the experience in farming and the skills needed to maintain a farm. Colleges today don't teach vocational skills that farming requires, like irrigation, mechanics, plumbing, electrical, construction, marketing, and putting in a hard day's work. The work ethic in this group has a lot to be desired. For a farmer, work comes first, and play later, if at all. The greenhorns need to remember that, in farming, it's all been done before; you just have to go out and do it! Plant it, grow it, pick it, sell it—there's nothing complicated about it. It's our job as experienced farmers to mentor this group and be available and accessible to them by offering internships and apprenticeships on our farms.

There is one last group that I would like to address that seems to always go unnoticed: the migrant worker. The backbone of American agriculture, whether it's industrial factory farms or small farms, migrant workers are the key element for most farms. Without them, US agriculture would crumble. Migrant workers are mostly from Mexico and the South American countries; of course, they come from other countries as well. They do the majority of the hard labor in agriculture. We could go on all day about the legals-versus-illegals debate, but the bottom line is that American agriculture needs migrant workers, or else we could not produce food in this country. Let me ask something of you. Whenever you're driving on an interstate highway, in any state, and you pass a field full of laborers picking a crop, take a close look at who's doing the work. Not the white guy in the air-conditioned cab of the $100,000 GPS-driven tractor, but the guy or gal in the hot sun stooped over planting, weeding, irrigating, or harvesting that crop. Safe to say it's a migrant worker. You don't see very many white boys doing that kind of work. That's reality, folks (and I'm a white guy, and my fourteen-year-old son is a white boy). As a matter of fact, think about all the crappy nonfarming jobs out there, like nurses' aides who clean bedpans in convalescent homes, maids changing sheets in motels, dishwashers in restaurants, masons, and landscapers. This work is done mostly by migrant workers trying to become citizens in this country, or at least trying to support their families in another country. The American white boys don't want to do these kinds of jobs; they want the cushy job, the high-paying CEO job. So next time you're voting to kick the illegal immigrants out of this country, just remember who's picking your food and wiping your ass when you get old. We had better figure out a way to create work visas for these people and keep them here, or we can't support this cart. Migrant workers are the spokes of the American labor wheel.

Today's small farmers are a diverse group of individuals that are producing fresh, local food and delivering it directly to the consumer. I ask you to consider the small farmers of today and the small farmers of tomorrow because they provide your food. We Americans need to improve the system for these small farmers to sustain themselves. Remember, farming makes up less than 1 percent of all occupations today, and only sixty years ago farmers made up about 10 percent of all of the occupations. Today less than 35 percent of all farmers claim farming as their primary source of income, and even more staggering is that the USDA notes that three-fifths of small farms have sales less than $10,000 a year. That's poverty level, folks! Hell, if you work for minimum wage flipping burgers at Wendy's you can make about $14,000 a year, plus you have a W-2 that can help you get a loan! We desperately need to find a way to build incentives for people to go into farming. We can't just paint a pretty picture for new farmers and then watch them fall on their faces.

But that's what the corporate and factory farms want. It would make their lives a lot easier if we weren't around. They are in the back pockets of the Farm Bill, and watch out for the next one because the USDA is proposing to create one hundred thousand "new farmers" out of the Farm Bill. New farmers. Beware of the wolf in sheep's clothing on this promise, because it's easy to get people fired up to start farming and then see 80 percent fail two years down the road because the system for small farmers sets us up to fail; it's built on false pretenses. We do need new farmers, but not at the expense of the small farm. We need to create a positive environment for the small farm to be sustainable by offering new farmers affordable land and resources and accessible financing for them and existing farmers. We also need to reduce the amount of regulation that limits farmers in making and distributing their products to the general public. We need to give them at least a fighting chance.

Chapter 9
WHERE DO WE GO FROM HERE?

As the farmer who won the lottery said when
asked what he was going to do with his winnings,
"Keep farming until it's all gone!"

~Unknown

All you have to do is ask the small farmer what needs to change and he or she will tell you: everything! As I stated in Chapter 6, the systems in this country are broken and currently they are set up for small farmers to fail, not to help create or sustain small farms. Anyone who grows or produces food impacts almost everything in our lives, so when we talk about solutions to help the small farmer in the twenty-first century we have to look at the whole picture. That picture includes not only what directly affects small farmers like taxes, land stewardship, marketing, and finances but also the American lifestyle, our economy, the food we eat, and how we view our overall heath. The media and our educators are the key to change. We must look at the small farmer in a different light in the twenty-first century.

The solutions depend on all of us knowing where our food comes from and making the right choices. We need to find solutions that will not only help the small farmers, but in doing so, will also make a healthier, more productive, and happier American. In the following chapters I call farmers and consumers to action. It's time that we not only talk about what needs to change, but make it happen! First and foremost, the small farmer and the consumer are the catalysts to change. To save, enhance, and create new small farms and farmers, we need the consumer's support. We need to take back our farms and rewrite systems in order to make a favorable and sustainable environment for small farms in the United States. There is a long road ahead of us small farmers, and we had better get busy!

Go Small or Not at All: Twenty-First Century Small Farms

Somehow we have to promote, enhance, and save our existing farms, and create a positive environment to attract more small farmers. We must take back our farms from government regulations, and change the slogan from the big corporate farms—"Get big or get out!"—to "Go small or not at all!" As farmers, we have to start with the customers within our communities, and have them demand fresh, local, organic, sustainable food systems from our elected officials. It all starts with the small farmer. No one else is going to cover our ass, so we must stand up and fight to stay alive. We must tell our politicians in our inner cities, suburbs, and rural communities to keep open space and affordable agricultural land available so that beginning farmers can get started, and existing ones can sustain their farms. My call to action is that we must develop our own food sovereignty—the right of people to define and protect their own food systems—starting at the local level. This is very similar to what Venezuela has done to save its food supply.

Venezuela has set the global model for food sovereignty, and we must begin to follow its model. In 1999, President Hugo Chávez said, "There is a food crisis in the world, but Venezuela is not going into that crisis. You can be sure of that!" At that time, the large corporate American agribusinesses were infiltrating countries, taking over regional agriculture homelands and polluting them with GMO crops that were to feed the world's population. In reality, what they did was ruin local agriculture in these countries, mostly in Europe and South America, by contaminating their heritage crops with GMO crops. And with their monocropping practices and mechanization, they denutrified the soils and put the locals out of work. President Chávez embraced the food sovereignty movement and, in 1999, changed Venezuela's constitution to bring back agriculture and to empower the citizens of Venezuela to control their food sources. A monumental article of the constitution shook the world. It states:

> Article 305: The state shall promote sustainable agriculture as the strategic basis for overall rural development. And consequently shall guarantee the population a secure food supply, defined as the sufficient and stable availability of food within the national sphere and timely and uninterrupted access to the same for consumers . . . Food production is in the national interest and is fundamental to the economic and social development of the Nation.

Article 306 followed, addressing rural development and support for agriculture activity; later Article 307 addressed land issues, establishing the basis for the passage of the "Law of the Land" in 2001, which simply states: "Agricultural land, first, and foremost, is for producing food, food for people." Before these changes to the constitution, 5 percent of the landowners owned 75 percent of the agricultural lands, most were corporate holdings, and 75 percent of the other agricultural landowners controlled only 6 percent of the land. As President Chávez began to reform the country's food sovereignty system, he banned all corporate agribusinesses and GMO crops in Venezuela, and began to give the land to the local small farmers. He set up the framework for food sovereignty, which is based on four major principles:

1. A food system free of corporate control, neoliberal economic policies, and unfair trade rules.
2. Building social and economic systems based on equality, social inclusion, shared wealth and resources, and participation of farmers. To return food production to the people through agrarian reform, cooperatively run farms, and food processing factories and facilities, as a basic human right rather than a commodity for profit.

3. Endogenous development, to promote development from within. This means valuing the local agricultural knowledge first as the fundamental element to their food sovereignty. To preserve Venezuela's native seeds, traditional farming methods, and culinary practices.

4. Participatory democracy. To empower the citizens of Venezuela to play a direct role in making food decisions that impact their lives. The use of community councils who monitor their food needs, shape food policy, and take control of their local food systems.

This bold approach has shown results. As of 2009, nearly 6.6 million acres have been returned to the stewardship of small local farmers, many of whom have organized themselves into cooperatives.

Venezuela has a proven record that its citizens value the small farmer and have their own food sovereignty, and we must do the same. Our land needs to be affordable and available to small farmers, and we must make low-interest financing and equity lines available for the small farmer, and affordable agricultural lands must be saved for future farmers to purchase to grow food. One way to do this is for local investors to work with local banks and credit unions to create small revolving lines of credit, let say under $50,000, that are sixty to seventy-two month loans backed by USDA and the Farm Service Agency (FSA). These loan concepts must be presented by farmers, farm co-op groups, and guilds to our legislators and incorporated into the Farm Bill, with state-by-state allocations. These loans should be low interest, say 4 percent or less, and available only to small farms that gross less than $100,000 per year.

Zoning laws must contain "right-to-farm" ordinances, so small parcels can have gardens, chickens, small livestock, and small commercial kitchens as well as processing facilities and storefronts to sell goods. We have to go back to the way it was not too long ago, when you could buy directly from the farmer. Bring back the milkman, the baker, the local butcher, the corner farmers' market (see Appendix A), and the farm stands. My call to action is for farmers to develop their own agriculture advisory boards, and become established in every county of their state, play an active role in land-use planning, and advise their local policymakers to enact "right-to-farm" ordinances that promote, enhance, and protect farmers and farmlands. Farmers need to be the leaders in the General Plan process in cities and counties, to set up ten- and twenty-year agricultural elements that explain how they are going to set up their own food sovereignty within their communities.

We must be able to sell directly to consumers from our farms. Farmers must be able to make a living from the farm itself; it is our "storefront." We as farmers must plan our farms. Time for a makeover! If you've been doing it the same way for years, it's time to take a new look at your farm. Start with Google Earth! Look at it from above and then from below (soils and water tests). I'm sure every farm can amend its farm to grow more things or diversify its operation. Look at the attributes of your farm. People love to visit farms and see the old buildings, or that heritage oak tree, the old broken windmill. Feature the history of your farm and be proud of what you do; boast about yourself by inviting the public to your farm. Farmers should have roadside stands, U-pick operations, CSAs, agritourism events like farm dinners, bed and breakfast inns, wine tastings, harvest festivals, mazes, pumpkin patches, hayrides, trail rides, and Christmas tree farms. The farm is how we package ourselves to the customer. Promote ordinances that don't restrict the small farmers' marketing ability to sell directly to the consumer. We need as many marketing avenues as possible to get our products directly to the consumer. Farmers and politicians must not give in to developers and residential pressure to take land out of agriculture and change it to residential and commercial zoning. Remember that asphalt and concrete cannot be used as a cover crop, and that all land left fallow, or as open space, can always be farmed. Asphalt and concrete are one-time crops that can't be reversed! Our zoning laws must be proagriculture for small farmers to survive, and they must be in the best interest of the small farmer.

We must make farming an attractive option for people as a small business. One way is to offer a certified sustainable farm program through community colleges, where a person interested in starting a small farm can attend a series of classes to learn about agricultural crops, crop production, farm business management, and marketing of goods. From there we must have apprenticeships, internships, and mentorships whereby people can get hands-on experience. Once they are on their own there must be some "beginner farmer" programs to get them started, like those from California FarmLink and the Farm Service Agency. Funding capital and operating capital must become available through local banks, credit unions, and our USDA and state farm-funding sources.

Another important element is to make farming more attractive—it all starts with image. Somehow we need to make farming more glamorous. We need more reality shows like *Farm Kings*, and to highlight more everyday farmers on YouTube. Don't always give the chefs the spotlight; make the farmer the rock star! Hell, we grow food for the chefs; they wouldn't have anything to cook if it wasn't for us. Farmers generally are shy, and that's why they farm; they just don't want to deal with people. They don't want to dress up to impress anyone, so old jeans or overalls and the same hat and old boots work just fine. Vegetable and fruit crops, along with pigs, cows, and sheep, don't talk back and as long as you feed and take care of them, all is good.

Americans are addicted to being entertained by visual and social media in all facets: television, computers, video games, iPads, iPods, smart phones, and cinema. The problem is that the mass media is run by corporate America. "Murdoch media" pretty much dictates what garbage we watch on TV. We need more public television, and there should be regulations set to allow free public advertising on all major networks. Today, the only businesses that can afford multimillion-dollar ads are the car, insurance, pharmaceutical, corporate fast food, and Wall Street companies. Main Street will never compete. That has to change. We need media grants from the USDA and state economic development grants for small farmers and businesses so that we get the same airtime as the corporate giants to promote buying local. The media is the major tool for change, and the 99 Percent Main Street has to take over the front seat and shove the 1 Percent Wall Street into the trunk. Farmers, let me tell you something, if we are going to survive in the twenty-first century we need to rock and roll and take center stage! I call on you to start putting your teenagers to work, not in the field (well, that too), but at what they're good at—all the electro-gadgets. Have them put together videos of fun things on your farm and post it on YouTube—that crazy trick your pig can do, or that fifty-pound cabbage you grew, or a day in the life of a farmer. Whatever, just get it out there. Get a Facebook page, and be active on Twitter. Work with your local television and radio stations. Most local counties televise their boring county supervisor meetings; hell, spice it up with a weekly session about what's in season, and do some local chef demonstrations videotaped from the farm. Hey, why not create your own local reality show? Think out of the box, get creative, and toot your own horn.

So as we positively change our image, how are we going to get people to like dirt? This is a hard one. The American public is so paranoid about germs. They are all about sanitizing everything! People need to go back to the earth, where all life begins and ends. Don't fight it! A little dirt under your fingernails is just fine. I don't know anyone who has died from eating a mouthful of organic soil. Let your kids make those mud pies and have those dirt-clod wars out in the empty lot. We need to bring back those old Tide commercials about the kids running into the house all dirty, but not from playing—

from farming! Have the kids come in the house in their dirty clothes, with bushels of vegetables for dinner, with their pet dog named "iPod." We have to change the perception of the farmer from a simple guy in overalls to that of an artist. Again, it's all about image and perception. Who is more important than a farmer who produces your food? As the bumper sticker reads, "NO FARMERS, NO FOOD." And no food, no you! I think it's about time that the American farmer gets recognized in *Time* magazine as the "Person of the Year"—matter of fact, it should be "Person of the Century"! No one has endured so much in the twentieth century as the small family farmer. As we continue into the twenty-first century we must stop this landslide against the small family farm.

We must take our small farms back by letting the farmers dictate what they need to survive. Again we must follow Venezuela's model of food sovereignty and make a commitment to support local food systems in our communities. We as Americans have to go back to the earth and connect our children and our grandchildren with it; we are all responsible for knowing our land and producing our own food. We need more educational documentaries about farming and farmers, and positive exposure of community food systems providing fresh, organic, healthy produce, meats, and dairy products to their local residents, schools, and institutions. The small American family farmer is making a comeback, and the big boys are on their heels. It's time to take back our small farms and put the big boys on their backs! Go farmer, go!

Do You Know Where Your Food Comes From?

Changing the image of farming starts with education. It starts with our children. We have to get our educators to start teaching kids the value of where their food comes from in kindergarten. Maybe the name should be changed to "kinder-*garden*," with the emphasis on gardens, gardening, and getting back to the earth, and learning about how important our small farmers are to the food chain. Educators have to get kids interested in soils, composting, beneficial insects, organic farming, worms, native plants, fruits, and vegetables at an early age, and not just by taking them on a stroll through the farmers' market. They must start preparing them to actually be able to garden and farm for themselves in the future. I think this is where farmers can take an active role in schools. For those of you who are my age (fifty-five), we can remember TV show characters like Captain Kangaroo and Mr. Green Jeans, who use to be on black-and-white television. We had an old Airline fourteen-inch TV in the den and in the mornings before school, Captain Kangaroo and Mr. Green Jeans would talk to the young school kids about vegetables and gardening and all the fun things about animals. That's what we need to bring back. Why not get retired and new young farmers to come to the schools to mentor young kids at an early age? Help them develop school gardens and grow food for their cafeterias. As they get older in middle and high school, there must be curriculum courses that deal with what I call "life skills," the simple things you are going to need to know in life. Kids need common-sense education on the basics of everyday living, and these simple courses would include balancing a bank account; debt management and how to not abuse credit; gardening and farming; vocational trades like mechanics, construction, welding, plumbing, and electrical; small business management and creating a business plan; home economics; and health, exercise, and nutrition. These are classes that would prepare our children for the real world, rather than classes that actually make them unemployable and degrees that don't lead to jobs. They get out in the real world and realize they have no skills. I truly believe that the American workforce has been trained by educators who lead them down the path of unemployment to "no-end" jobs, with nowhere else to go. This is only adding to the statistics of economic woes. Ask any farmer and they will tell you that you can read all the books about farming you want, but until you get down and dirty, and put in a farmer's day of work, you will never truly understand where your food comes from. Every school should maintain a garden; let the children pick the fresh fruits and vegetables to be added into their school lunches. We don't need the corporate sponsorship from Coca-Cola to have soda machines in every hallway, or the corporate corn giants dictating that there must be GMO-derived high-fructose corn syrup in every meal. Parents, stand up and fight for your kids to eat healthy in schools!

A vital part of education lacking today is that of experience. We as a society spend more time learning than doing. Kids need to spend more time out of the classroom and away from the video games, texting, and television, and more time experiencing life skills. Most farmers would agree that we should lower the working age for teens from sixteen to fourteen years of age. Teenagers need to learn good work habits and ethics early in their teens, not when they are eighteen or nineteen when they get their first job. Allowing kids to work at fourteen would keep them off the streets, help prevent them from getting into gangs, allow them to make their own money, and contribute income to financially stressed families. There are many small farmers who would love to employ young teens and teach them working skills that they can use later in life. High schools should incorporate work-study time into the curriculum, whereby students actually work at a local small farm or business for four to eight hour per week and get credit for their time. In truth, we could actually have Future Farmers of America (FFA) again, which still exists but only in rural communities around the country.

It doesn't stop at just educating our children; we must do a better job at educating the general public as to where our food actually comes from, and what we are actually eating. Thanks to the organic and "buy local" movements over the last few years, and books from Michael Pollan such as *The Omnivore's Dilemma* and *In Defense of Food*, movies like *Food, Inc.*, and TV hosts like Oprah Winfrey and Dr. Oz, people are educating themselves about good, wholesome, organic, fresh, local foods.

It shows in the attendance and increasing popularity of farmers' markets. More people want to know where their food comes from, but there still is more we can do. Farmers should become mentors, educating the general public about where our food comes from, and fill in the gap in farming knowledge that comes with current and past generations. Farmers must make an effort to bring interns to their farm to teach them the ropes of farming and ranching, and make an effort to have school kids visit their farms.

In doing my part, every spring I teach a native plants class and a sustainable agriculture class at Feather River College in Quincy, California, and at Sierra College in Truckee, California. These short courses are a nice introduction for students, but I wanted to take it even further, so in 2013, we set up a Sustainable Agriculture Work Study Program, whereby five to six students will be under my supervision to work a variety of farms this summer for credit and a stipend. For every forty-five hours of fieldwork, they will receive one unit of credit, with six credits maximum. In addition, they will receive a fifty-dollar stipend for every unit of credit. The majority of their fieldwork will consist of crop planning, crop production, harvesting, and postharvest duties and food safety, along with marketing and integrated pest and nutrition management. For my compensation, the Feather River College pays me $1,500 that I will use to pay the stipend. In return I get student labor for my farm and the opportunity to mentor these students.

This book is also my first attempt to bring awareness to the general public about life as a small farmer, and the influences and impacts we directly have on American society. I plan to publish a sequel, *July & Winter: The Growing Seasons of the Sierra for Farmers and Gardeners* in 2014, detailing gardening and farming methods for the Sierra Nevada region.

The next part of the education process involves educating consumers about what's in their food. It's all about food labeling and reading the labels on the food products we buy at the grocery store. Currently, the USDA does not require conventional (nonorganic) farms to notify the public of any chemicals, GMO crops, or pesticides that have been sprayed or applied to our food. That's scary! You might ask yourself, really? Just look at the labels on your processed food packages; the large corporations have diverted the American public to become more aware of the nutrients, or lack of, and the fats, carbohydrates, sodium, calories, and the high-fructose corn syrup than all the pesticides they sprayed on it. And for produce, there are no labels at all. It's amazing that the general public has been so complacent on this issue. Most people don't realize all the chemicals that our conventional produce comes into contact with on a daily basis. Ever wonder why every piece of fruit looks exactly the same way, same color and size, and why they are all shiny? *That doesn't happen in nature.* A lot of chemicals come into contact with your conventional produce to make them look, taste, and smell the same way. Some of these chemicals include cleaning agents and solvents from processing plants along with wax to make the fruit shiny and to close their pores so they last longer. Also, gases of nitrogen and carbon dioxide are injected into the room to ripen your fruit so they all look the same, nice and juicy—then you bite into them and they taste like cardboard.

Have you ever noticed that there isn't an aroma of fresh produce in the produce section of your major chain grocery store? Why is that? Because all the fruit is picked green and placed in cold storage for months, there is very little sugar and starch, which give out an aroma as they ripen and break down naturally. When all this fruit is gassed, it ripens exponentially at the same time, and it gives color but no flavor. Now walk through a farmers' market in prime season of peaches, plums, and melons and you can really smell them—there is no comparison!

As for pesticides, there are so many applied to conventional produce that I can spend a whole book on that subject. So I'll just give you enough information to scare you. A "pest" is anything you don't want, and "cide" is anything that will kill it. The category of pesticides include fungicides (kills pathogens), rodenticides (kills rodents), herbicides (kills weeds), avicides (kills birds), insecticides (kills insects), miticides (kills mites and spiders), algicides (kills algae), molluscicides (kills snails and slugs), and nematocides (kills wormlike organisms that feed on roots). These are just a few pesticides that are applied to conventional fruits and vegetables. Most are man-made, derived from petroleum-based and pharmaceutical industries. Most pesticides are tested on laboratory animals and rated by lethal dose (LD rating) as to the harmful effects to the person applying the pesticide only, not to the environment. In nature some compounds break down quickly, and some persist for years and can be passed on through the food chain, as did DDT in the 1960s, a topic that Rachel Carson's book *Silent Spring* exposed the world. The USDA and FDA register and regulate all pesticides. All conventional farmers must complete annual pesticide-use reports for all pesticides used, but they are not required to name these pesticides or GMO crops on your produce or processed foods. This is where the system disconnects with the consumer. Consumers must demand that they have the right to know what goes into their food! Tell your legislators, write letters to the USDA and the FDA and watchdog groups like Food and Water Watch, and demand that you want all pesticides and GMO crops labeled on your food!

Fertilizers and other soil amendments are not classified as pesticides; they are a whole other animal. Most are petroleum-based components of nitrogen, phosphorous, and potassium, the major nutrient needs of a plant. There are two types: fast release and slow release, which means the release of nutrients available to a plant. Fast-release fertilizers are heavy nitrogen and phosphorous feeders that break down quickly in the soil according to water and soil temperature. The warmer the soil, and the more water available, the faster they feed. Most last about thirty days of feeding on the crop. What happens most of the time is that these fertilizers release more nitrogen than the plant can intake; thus it leaches through the soil and ends up in our groundwater and rivers, causing nitrate and phosphorous problems that can create algal blooms in lakes and pollute open waterways. Slow-release fertilizers are different and usually have some kind of coating over the pellet, a sulfur-based product, or even a biodegradable plastic or cellulose coating that breaks down slowly, releasing small amounts of fertilizer at a time to minimize leaching, and lasts anywhere from two to eight months. In addition to causing nitrate and phosphorous problems in our waterways, the heavy application of man-made fertilizers, along with pesticides, are depleting our soils of natural organic matter and killing our soil microbes to the point that our soils no longer have the structure to sustain themselves and are eroding and blowing away. The Natural Resources Conservation Service (NRCS) documents that we are losing millions of tons of topsoil every year due to industrial agriculture's conventional monocropping agriculture practices. In organic agriculture, all man-made pesticides and fertilizer amendments are banned from use. In organics, the only pesticides used are natural and biological compounds like oils, waxes, pheromones, traps, soaps, and the use of beneficial insects. As for fertilizers, the nutrients for plants are provided from compost, worm castings, manures, and cover crops.

The organic certification movement started around 1970, when a group of organic farmers wanted to standardize a pure process of growing food without using man-made, toxic fertilizers or pesticides. To get their foot in the door and achieve public acceptance, this group, California Certified Organic Farmers (CCOF), bowed to pressure from conventional farming groups and agreed to prove that no synthetic products would be used in their farming practices by way of inspections, recordkeeping, an operations plan, labeling the products organic and including ingredients on the label, and paying absurd fees for certification by a neutral party. In return, the conventional farmers, large and small, got away scot-free, spraying and applying toxic fertilizers and pesticides to your fruits and vegetables at will, and not telling you a thing! That still continues today! Consumers, WAKE UP! Just remember that when you buy that peach at a supermarket, you might as well take a booklet of chemicals that have been sprayed on that peach home and read it to your children as a bedtime story. Will you feel good about what's in that peach that you're feeding your child? I think not. I guarantee you that you will only eat organic produce and food products after reading that list. The sad part of this is that there is no real way to know what was sprayed on any conventional nonorganic produce because disclosure is not required. The general public is only safe if they buy organic foods because buying organic insures you that no synthetic pesticides, fertilizers, or GMO crops were used on the produce that you bought.

We, as a public, have to educate ourselves about where our food comes from, and that goes for our meats and processed foods too. The common complaint that I hear most is that organic is too expensive. For those of you trying to decide to go organic, try and take this approach. I know there is only so much money that you can spend on trying to feed a family, and that the argument of "I just can't afford it" doesn't hold water. Like Mom always said, "Mr. Can't never did anything," and that's true in this case. Aside from the obvious that it's better for you than conventional produce, studies show that organic produce has five to ten times more nutritional value than conventional produce, so you can start out by buying less. It will cost you about the same to buy smaller portions of organic as larger portions of conventional, plus you're not paying for the pesticides. Cut out the most toxic conventional produce, including apples, strawberries, broccoli, cauliflower, and out-of-season, out-of-country fruit (there is no telling what's been done when it's grown in another country), and buy those organic. Next, try and attend a farmers' market at least once a month and just buy seasonal fruits and vegetables. (You can search for farmers' markets in the United States at www. localharvest.org.) If there are no organic growers, or you don't want to pay their prices, talk to a small conventional farmer about what he or she uses on the crops. Most of the time, small growers don't spray pesticides because they are very expensive, and they don't grow enough volume to justify going organic. Farmers love to talk about how they grow their crops. If your work schedule doesn't allow you to attend farmers' markets, look for a CSA box, the subscription program that delivers a box of fresh produce to your door weekly through the growing season. There are many ways to begin to provide healthier options for your family. The best way to educate yourself about where your food comes from is to get to know your local small farmers or ranchers and ask them yourself at your local farmers' market. Again, farmers take great pride in the fruits, vegetables, and meats they grow and raise. They usually can't shut up about their products—I know I can't. There is no better satisfaction to a farmer than for a customer to be interested in his or her farming techniques, because every small farmer says, "Ours is the best because I grew it and picked myself; no one knows it better than me." It just doesn't get any better than that!

One Size Doesn't Fit All: Taxes, Fees, Rules, and Subsidies

Where do I begin with taxation? First, the IRS has to change the Schedule F form, or what I call the "*F*—— your farmer" form. Lenders must consider gross earnings for financing purposes, and net earnings must continue to be the taxable income, based on itemized deductions. So how do you change the IRS? Good question. It has to start with a large lobby group like the Farm Bureau. We need a petition to circulate through all Farm Bureau chapters. As much as I think they are in the special interest of corporate American and the biotech industries, they are our only hope for the little guy. We must bring it to the attention of our local mayors and Boards of Supervisors, then on to our legislatures to take it to Congress, and then on to the Senate. Farmers need tax reform at all levels. This would be a major undertaking by the small farm community, but it can be done. Here is one way to attract farmers: make all small farmers with gross sales under $100,000 exempt from income tax. We're at the poverty level anyway; why not exempt us?

We as farmers have to be able to comfortably find financing and equity lines at low interest to begin, sustain, and expand our farming operations. The sales tax issue is usually set up by each state. With the diverse amount of products that farmers use, some states have a reduced sales tax for farmers, usually around 4 percent. Farmers need this break. The consumer doesn't pay sales tax on produce and groceries, so why do farmers have to pay sales tax on products they use to grow your food? Farmers should be exempt from sales tax on agricultural products.

The next issue is property taxes. Based on my experience, agricultural lands are appraised at about 40 percent of the value of residential and commercial properties, yet we are assessed "city-like" property taxes. There should be a reduced formula for farmers on agriculture-zoned properties. Approach your local tax assessor's office, and push your Board of Supervisors to look into a reduced formula for all agricultural-zoned properties. In addition, certified agricultural producers (anyone who makes income off of farming) should be entitled to enter a Williamson Act contract with their county if they farm twenty acres or more. This would allow a huge percentage of small farmers to get a reduced property tax break and create an incentive for young people to go into farming. The Williamson Act contracts are also set up county by county in the state of California, based on a minimum of one hundred acres (althought this varies by county). There is no reason that counties can't amend the Williamson Act to reduce minimums to forty or even twenty acres, depending on the sizes of that county's productive agricultural producers' parcels. In areas where there are a lot of large acreages for cattle grazing, one hundred acres is sufficient, but in counties that have smaller agricultural land producing vegetables and fruit crops, twenty or forty acres is more realistic. If everyone is farming on forty acres or less, what good is a one hundred-acre minimum Williamson Act?

Last is the estate tax issue. Over the past fifty years it's been really sad to watch farmers work all their lives to build their farms and then lose them. As they get older, all they want to do is leave their farms for their children, but the probate laws and estate taxes have ruined families and have seriously contributed to the decline in family farms. In today's world, it is very important that all farmers make time for estate planning to save their farms. All families should put together a living trust, so that when the time comes all parties are taken care of securely. Don't wait until it's too late. See your attorney or find a competent estate planner to put this document together. Most small farms can be saved with a little planning. In the future, it would be nice to have farmers exempt from estate taxes if the property is being left to a family member, because agricultural land values are known to be considerably less than residential and commercial properties. Most small farms fall under the probate laws and are not exempt from inheritance tax. When Nonno died, we paid the price by not having a living trust set up—a document put together by a family lawyer before someone dies that tells the heirs exactly what they are going to receive and avoids the hassle of going through probate—and it nearly ruined our family because Dad and his sisters had to pay off the inheritance taxes, causing bad blood among the siblings that just about folded the flower farm. We were one of the few that survived inheritance taxes. Farmers should be able to pass on the farm to their children without the fear of the kids having to sell the family farm to pay the estate taxes. That's just plain wrong, so do your homework ahead of time.

How about those rules and regulations? There's parity, and then there's parity. One size doesn't fit all, and bigger isn't better. Common sense must return to the rules and regulations for small farmers. Strict rules and regulations must be placed on the large corporate factory farms to protect food safety, the consumer, the field worker, and the environment we live in because what they do can affect thousands of people and whole communities. But the small farmer is the "little fish in the big pond"; common-sense laws are all we need for them. As I mentioned earlier small farmers are not on the same playing field as the large conglomerates. Most small farmers sell their produce direct to the consumer in small amounts, just like picking it from your garden and bringing it into the kitchen to prepare a meal for that evening. Ridiculous environmental health laws about sampling at farmers' markets, cooking outside for a farm dinner, or setting up an on-farm commercial kitchen should instead be boilerplate, common-sense laws that don't cost farmers an arm and a leg.

As for the food safety rules and regulations, why does the farmer always get blamed for the *E. coli* outbreak in packaged spinach or lettuce? Small farmers have been picking lettuce and spinach for hundreds of years and eating it right out of the fields, dirty hands and all, so why all of a sudden in the last ten years is it becoming a problem? I have my theory. First, quit feeding corn to cows. As I said earlier, cows weren't meant to eat corn; they're meant to eat grass. They can't efficiently digest corn to get rid of the *E. coli* bacteria. So quit it! Second, I believe the problem with bacteria starts in the packing plants, not with the farmers. Have you ever visited a factory that prepackages spring mix and spinach? I did, and was amazed at what a piece of lettuce goes through to get packaged. It's mechanically picked, thrown on a conveyer belt, transferred to bins, trucked to cold storage, trucked to a packaging plant, washed, mixed, re-washed, blow-dried, spin-dried, tumbled, waxed, blown into packages, sealed, boxed, refrigerated, and shipped to distributors, and then stores. After all this no wonder the lettuce gets slimy after a few days in the fridge. I would too if I had to go through all that.

Inside the plant it's hot and humid, with hundreds of workers and a lot of warm water residues—a perfect environment for bacteria to breed. I feel that *E. coli* comes from these packaging plants because bacteria can grow in a matter of hours under the right conditions. How are they going to track it? We started growing spring mix at Sierra Valley Farms about thirteen years ago. We tried the prewashed, prepackaged spring mix bags like Earthbound Farm uses, but when we tumbled it and washed it and spun it, we could never get it dry, no matter how long we spun it. It would not last more than three to four days in a bag and the process actually tore the larger leaves of spinach and lettuces. We realized that lettuce is 90 percent water, and by growing it organically, in a harsher outside environment, the cell walls of the plant tissue become thicker and healthier, and help protect the leaf from breaking down when handled. The less you handle leafy greens, the longer they last. We wash our hands, pick our greens with a kitchen knife before noon while it's cool, lightly tumble out the weeds and any debris, dry package it in ziplock bags, and put it into the cooler. We sell it as a fresh pick, not as a prewash mix. It's off to the farmers' market the next day, and our "world-famous" greens are known to last up to three weeks in the crisper! Knock on wood since we have sold over one hundred thousand bags of greens this way over the years and so far not one problem, because it's a "fresh pack." No washing involved. When you add "foreign" water, you invite bacteria to form. That's my story, and I'm sticking to it!

If "leafy green safety regulations"—like the prepackaging steps mentioned above—are imposed on the small farmer it will put every small vegetable grower at the farmers' market out of business. We cannot conform to the requirements the USDA is mandating. Impose them on the large factory farms because those packaging plants are where the problems begin. For the small farmer, it's common sense: wash your hands, keep things clean, and rinse the dirt off your root vegetables.

As far as processing foods, farmers should be able to use small commercial kitchens to make their value-added products—

pretty simple. A paper trail is created so that you can track the product and establish expiration dates for each item. It's not that difficult. Local environmental health departments need to streamline these procedures to make it user-friendly for farmers to make value-added products like jams, jellies, pickles, and other condiments.

Another thing we desperately need is major reform in the rules and regulations for small farmers and ranchers to process and sell their own dairy and meat products. What the state and federal regulators impose on factory farms has no place at small dairy and meat producers. It's all about animal density and concentration of animal waste, pretty simple. Factory farms put a lot of animals in a small area that create large concentrated amounts of animal waste. Small farmers have a few animals in a large area and can disperse the animal waste. Apples and oranges here, folks! We need to pressure our wonderful USDA officials and the Farm Bureau, and demand that our legislators change the direction they are taking with the meat and dairy industry. We need USDA grants for more mobile slaughter trailers, meat packing plants, and small dairy processing plants with funded inspectors, so that the small dairies and meat producers can be back in business. We need to reduce the rules and regulations for these small producers so that the general public can buy their raw milk, cheese, yogurt, cream, packaged meats, processed meats, baked goods, and eggs direct from local farmers and ranchers. Small producers should not be treated like criminals. Presently, regulators place such large fees and constraints against small farmers before they even get started, as if they have done something wrong, and discourage the "buy local" movement by placing major impositions against local farmers with these regulations. Impose the strict regulations on the violators, the large factory farms, who dump waste into our streams and rivers and perform inhumane practices of animal husbandry, and leave the small farmer alone.

The final piece of the puzzle is to restructure the subsidy program for farmers. It all begins with gutting the Farm Bill. Get rid of it as it stands today. Like I said earlier, small farmers don't receive any subsidies; only the major commodity corporations receive billions of dollars to plant or not plant crops according to the global demand of the commodity. The subsidized commodities are: rice, corn, wheat, soybean, and cotton; the rest get diddly-squat! We need to rename it the Small Farm Bill, because big corporate farms don't need subsidies; the small farmer does. The lobbyists of large corporations like Cargill, biotech giants like Monsanto, and insurance companies like the Farm Bureau are in the back pockets of our politicians to make sure the corporate farms get richer and the small farms get poorer! That's right, it's been a long time that we've been taking it in the shorts, and it's time for a Farm Bill handout. I'm not proud; I'll take farmer food stamps and go on farmer welfare! The structure of the bill should be focused on helping the small farmer. Yes, there is a need to support the global food market and these corporate farms do play a part in our food system, but it shouldn't be at the expense of the small farmer. The small farmer is Main Street, and the corporate farmer is Wall Street. We would get a bigger bang for our buck by subsidizing and investing in the small farmer. We'd keep our money at home and help stimulate our local economies, not some sweatshop in China processing garlic to sell to the United States.

This is another monumental task at hand for the small farmer. How is the small farmer ever going to get priority from the federal, state, and local governments to help subsidize capital investment for new, young, and old farmers to buy land and equipment, and go into farming? In the twenty-first century that is going to be the major stumbling block for farmers. This should be high priority and I call all farmers to action! Every farm group needs to get on board with this train. That includes: the Farm Bureau, farm cooperatives, fruit and vegetable associations, organic certifiers like CCOF, Oregon Tilth, and Quality Assurance International, and county and state agriculture commissioners and boards. We need to lobby our legislators, through agriculture associations, labor unions, and farmers actually becoming politicians to revamp the subsidies system so that they help small farmers who gross under $100,000 per year. They are the ones that need it. We need to infiltrate government and have an influence! Those subsides should be for land purchases and leases, operating capital, capital improvements, farming technology improvements, irrigation efficiency, and energy efficiency on solar, wind, biodiesel, and geothermal projects.

In addition, subsidies should come from the large conventional corporations in the form of a tax, which is then used to subsidize small organic farmers as a reward for doing the right thing, growing organically. The subsidies should reward small farmers for their good stewardship of the land and sustainable farming practices, instead of rewarding large farms for investing in GMO crops, applying poisonous pesticides, employing monoculture farming practices, and polluting our soils and the environment. The large corporate farms should be assessed an "environment tax" for polluting our food, land, water, and air, and that tax should subsidize (reward) small farmers. The new bill must subsidize all specialty crops, including fruits and vegetables, not the large commodities of corn, rice, wheat, soybean, and cotton. We need to subsidize the specialty-crop farmers; California alone provides the United States nearly half its fruits, nuts, and vegetables. We need subsidies to create more organic farmers that can provide healthy fruits and vegetables so that we can reduce health problems and cancer. It all starts with the Farm Bill when it comes to providing subsidies, or any funding for farmers, and we just got screwed again with the 2012 Farm Bill. It's business as usual: conglomerates like Cargill get their subsidies, the rest goes to food stamps, and they'll throw small farmers a bone—a few insignificant conservation programs to make them look good. Now, and every eight years following, small farmers around the country have to get up in arms, stand up for their cause, and get it in the Farm Bill. Something has to change!

Reduce Our Footprint: Stewards of the Land

As small farmers, we are the ultimate stewards of the land, examples of the true meaning of sustainability. If you look up the USDA's legal definition of sustainable agriculture, in the US Code Title 7, Section 3103, it is defined as an integrated system of plant and animal production practices having a site-specific application that will over the long term: (1) satisfy human food and fiber, (2) enhance environmental quality and the natural resources based upon which the agricultural economy depends, (3) make the most efficient use of nonrenewable resources and on-farm resources, (4) sustain the economic viability of farm operations, and (5) enhance the quality of life for farmers and society as a whole. The problem is that it says nothing about what sustainability is really all about, which is best put by the magazine *American Small Farm and Country Life* (www.smallfarm.com): sustainable agriculture is a method of farming that is not only humane, and ecologically and socially ethical, but can sustain itself, and puts back into the earth what it takes out, making a cycle requiring no inputs from the outside.

For comparison, consider conventional factory farming's use of petroleum-based synthetic fertilizers versus organic farming's use of composted animal manures. The latter method is sustainable, and in general, is the practice of most small farmers. If you look at the USDA's definition of sustainable agriculture, it says nothing about what is humane or ethical, renewable resources, or being responsible stewards of the land. It basically says that we must satisfy food needs by efficiently using nonrenewable resources (petroleum-based products) as long as we can, and protect the environment only if it's in the best interest of the agricultural economy to sustain these farming operations and enhance the quality of life as a whole. But at what expense? Industrial farming is not sustainable; we are going to run out of nonrenewable resources someday. It says nothing about utilizing renewable resources with no inputs from the outside. That is the key to sustainability—renewable resources and no inputs from the outside. The USDA definition is not sustainable, folks!

We small farmers must take the responsibility to minimize our footprint on the world. We must be the leaders in renewable energy, organic farming, and environmental stewardship. All farms should strive to have their own source of power by utilizing biodiesel, wind, solar, and/or hydroelectric power. There needs to be a push by the agricultural community to provide grants, subsidies, and more energy reimbursement programs for small farmers to fund these power plants and recycling initiatives. Utility rates are running us out of business and not allowing us to retrofit our farms for renewable energy. We are in the twenty-first century, and with all the technology available you can't tell me that we can't have solar-powered and electric tractors and small equipment. All new tractors should be equipped for biodiesel use, and have an electric option. As for the automobile industry, it's a joke! No small farmer wants a 400-horsepower, fifteen-miles-per-gallon, custom-cab "gas hog" that costs $45,000 and can back itself into a parking stall. We are not going to pay that kind of money for this truck. We don't want it! Get rid of it. It does us no good! We want a small Toyota pickup—eight-foot bed, with a one-ton payload, stripped of all the electronic bullshit—that gets fifty miles to the gallon and costs $16,000 or less. I'll even put the CD player in it! Why, I could even find a repossessed house in my community for $50,000 and put wheels on it. The auto industry has got to get real!

Small farmers need options that will help us reduce our footprint on this earth. We need some practical engineering to help the 99 Percent. Setting up recycling programs alone can create hundreds of jobs within communities for green-waste management, and it will reduce our footprint on landfills. The prisons are overcrowded, and what better use of a labor force than for our green-waste/composting operations and recycling plants—have workers separate glass, aluminum, plastic, and paper from our landfills. We have a long way to go in our communities to reduce our footprint. We're a consume-and-dispose-of society in America; everything is used and abused, and thrown away. As small farmers we can begin to work with our communities to try and break this habit, but it's not going to be easy. Americans have to understand that small farming operations not only use less fossil fuel to produce their fresh, organic, local food but also use less to package them, less to advertise and market them in plastic labels and sign boards, and less in transporting them hundreds of miles by truckers and distributors to supermarkets.

Organic farmers in particular reduce our footprint on Earth by farming with natural cycles that happen in nature. We utilize crop diversity, composting, cover cropping, and crop rotations for our nutrient and pest management programs, and land stewardship for our natural resource conservation efforts to sustain our farms. The industrial factory farms utilize nonrenewable practices of monoculture and fossil-fueled pesticides, fertilizers, heavy equipment, and long-range transporting, along with a heavy consumption of electric power, fuel, and water resources, thus producing large amounts of waste by-products. This is not sustainable, and they leave quite a footprint that is depleting our soils and polluting our natural resources. We need to reduce our footprint, and it all begins at home and in our local communities. We're not going to change overnight, but we have to begin now if we are going to sustain not only small farms but our society as a whole.

Buy Local—Put Up or Shut Up: Building Local Economies

Once farmers are established it is crucial that the local communities support these farmers by buying direct from these farms. There has to be a commitment from the community to buy everything these farmers can grow. There has been a big push in the last few years to "buy local," to support your local businesses, which puts money back into your community to boost the local economy. We all know that the average piece of fruit travels about 1,500 miles to get to your table, so you it makes sense to buy from your local farmers at the farmers' market, or to subscribe to a weekly CSA box. The number of farmers' markets in the US has seen a steady rise, increasing an average of about 7.5 percent per year since 1994, indicating that people want to know where their food comes from and support local farmers and vendors. There seems to be another economic element that goes along with the buy-local movement, and that is: "I will buy local as long as I can afford it, and if I can't find it cheaper anywhere else."

About ten years ago the buy-local movement began around California, and five years ago it really hit the Reno/Lake Tahoe area, when restaurants and the resort industry were booming, farmers' market attendance was on the rise, and everyone wanted to buy locally made or grown products. Here at Sierra Valley Farms, we couldn't keep up with restaurant demand for locally grown, fresh, organic vegetables. Plumas and Sierra Counties were on board as well, trying to convince county residents to buy local. Posters were stuck on every business window, and plastered all over the local newspapers. It got to the point that words like "buy local" and "sustainable" were interchangeable catchphrases that were very marketable. If you said that you were a "sustainable" business or restaurant using "fresh, organic" produce/products from "local farmers," you were swamped with customers. But something fishy was going on, because when economic woes started a few years ago restaurants and small stores kept promoting themselves as buying from local farmers, but us small farmers have seen a decline in local sales to restaurants and small natural food stores. The public says they are buying local from the mom-and-pop stores and eating at the local restaurants, but the major chains are seeing an increase in their annual sales while more and more local storefronts are becoming vacant. We need to face reality, folks: economics is the bottom line for most consumers and business owners. In hard economic times we can "push" buy local all we want, but if Sysco has organic stewed tomatoes at half the price offered by the local farmers, most chefs will go the cheaper route. In most cases, the public won't know the difference at the restaurant, or in the recipe; the only one that suffers is the small farmer because he or she didn't get the sale, but the restaurateur benefits from advertising on the menu that they buy fresh, organic produce from local farmers.

I can say from experience that most chefs couldn't care less about buying from small farmers; they have their set menus, and it's too easy for them to sit in their warm and fuzzy offices and pick up the phone and have every kind of produce available at their fingertips from these big distributors. Who cares if it comes from five hundred miles away; the chef is only going to cook it anyway. It's sad to say, but it's the truth—very few chefs have even been to the farmers' market, or out to my farm, and I can say only a handful live and breathe the "buy local" concept; the rest just ride its coattails and reap from the benefits while serving you the same ingredients that go to Denny's. There is a code of ethics to be followed here. Misleading the general public can be very disruptive to a buy-local movement you are trying to adhere to in a small community. So, to all of you businesses claiming fame about buying local, are you putting your money where your mouth is? And to the consumer, I ask you to put up or shut up about buying local. Are you actually buying local versus going to the major chain stores like Costco, Walmart, WinCo, Lowe's, or Home Depot? I know most people do occasionally frequent these stores for items they can't find locally, but you have to ask yourself, "Have I made a conscious effort to buy locally and keep my dollars in my community? What can I do to help bring businesses in to fill those voids?"

Despite economic woes, we do have to stick to our guns and buy local in order to bring back small farms and businesses.

Plain and simple, we have to change the way we do business. It goes back to putting a little more effort into making that sale to a small farmer, or supporting that small café down the street. For most Americans, they will take the easy way out, the path of least resistance. If they can go to Walmart twenty miles away and get produce, house plants, janitorial supplies, and office supplies, and catch a quick "burger" at the Burger King, why go see Fred, Tom, Sally, or Jim and run all over town to get a few items from their local stores? Americans want convenience! We as small farmers and business owners have to convince the public it's better to buy local. Chefs and produce buyers for small natural food stores and co-ops have to realize that produce picked fresh yesterday and delivered to you today has tons more nutrition, flavor, and freshness than the shipment you're getting on Friday from UNFI (United Natural Foods Inc.), Bonanza, or Veritable Vegetable. Plus, you don't even know who picked it and when, let alone what shape it will be in when it gets to your door. Come on people, you've got to get on board with this buy local thing and be serious about it, or small farms and businesses will become extinct. Shopping at Walmart and Costco is just putting more money into the 1 Percent Wall Street and taking from the 99 Percent Main Street. You're cutting your own throats!

How can we get the consumer and businesses to work together to support each other's needs? I call to action the local consumer and local businesses and farmers to come to a common ground. It's a catch-22, as most consumers, if they had a choice, want a "one-stop shop," where they can get everything they want at the same place, for the cheapest price and the best value. Local businesses want most people to buy their products for the best price, and depend on return customers to sustain their businesses. In small communities, what frequently happens is that there isn't enough diversity among businesses where the customer can shop. There is too much duplication of nondemand stores. How many thrift stores, secondhand stores, antique stores, pawnshops, dog- and cat-grooming stores, psychic readings, and ministorage places does one community need? I think local chambers of commerce and downtown merchants should plan their communities so that the locals can get what they need right in town, the basics: healthy food, clothing, repair shops, good restaurants, secure schools, local hospital and medical centers, insurance, electronics, and more. As for the locals, they have to commit to supporting the local businesses, bottom line. In most cases I don't see them doing it; for some reason they drift to the large chains like Walmart, Home Depot, and WinCo, which eventually kills the downtown merchants. We've all seen it.

One thing that the big chains can't offer the public is customer service. The staff at those stores are "just a number." They just want to put in their eight hours and go home; there is no loyalty. Instead, local businesses and us small farmers kill you with kindness! It's *all* about customer service. The farmer knows his product, and the customer is always right. If that peach isn't right, give them another one: "It's on me!" You can't do that at Costco. That's the value of buying local, knowing the farmer or small business owner, knowing what you're getting, and cultivating friendships along the way. As long as you support that small farmer, he or she will continue to go to that farmers' market, or drop produce off at your restaurant and have a beer at the bar or bite to eat after work. It's a win-win for everyone: you support me (farmer), and I'll send people to your restaurant or store to shop.

On the business side of things, I can't stress enough how important it is for businesses, customers, and local communities to go out of their way and make buying local a priority. Chefs need to change their permanent menus and put together seasonal menus featuring seasonal produce sourced from local farmers. Chefs have to make that commitment, and I don't see it happening in the Reno/Tahoe area restaurants. The same goes for farmers as well. They have to think out of the box, and go out of their way to work with chefs, and produce buyers, to accommodate their needs and be more flexible, understand deadlines, and make seasonal produce available to them. It's spokes in a wheel, folks. Just remember that if you put Sierra Valley Farms' name on the menu, you had better be serving my spring mix—I will know if it's iceberg lettuce from Bonanza produce.

One big challenge of the "buy local" movement for small farmers is getting fresh-picked produce to the consumer. The customer must have access to that fresh produce. Even though the number of farmers' markets increases each year, based on my calculations of USDA figures, California's population, and estimated attendance at its 730 farmers' markets and use of a CSA program at the time I wrote this book, only 5 percent of Californians have access to local produce and products and buy directly from farmers. That's pathetic! That means 95 percent of the public are buying from superstores like Safeway, WinCo, Albertsons, Raley's, and Walmart. Soon these farmers' markets are going to be saturated by small farmers competing for space and there will be no other avenues to sell freshly grown, local produce. The public needs more avenues, more ways to buy fresh produce directly from the farmers.

Currently, the food distribution system works two ways, as I stated earlier: factory-farm mass distribution, and buying direct from the farmer. There is nothing in between. For the buy-local movement to work it has to be a community effort. Buying local isn't just the individual buying a peach at the farmers' market; it's everybody buying that peach from that farmer. That includes restaurants, food stores, hospitals, school cafeterias, convalescent homes, food banks, jails, prisons, and households.

In Truckee, California, there is a community effort to make the town of Truckee the "healthiest town in America." It's a grassroots effort spearheaded by Dr. Dan Smith of the Genesa Living Foundation that puts fresh, local, organic foods into school lunch programs and provides education to the Truckee/ Tahoe region on living a healthy lifestyle (www.genesaliving. com). Examples like this are going to change the way we eat, live, and make healthier choices for our communities. All food establishments must have access to the small farmer's fresh-picked, organic, seasonal produce and products.

One concept that is becoming popular is the concept of a food hub, where farmers drop off their produce and people and businesses come by to purchase them. A couple of hubs are being created in northern California and Nevada, one by Great Basin Community Food Co-op in Reno, Nevada (www.DROPP.coop), and the other, Tahoe Food Hub (www. tahoefoodhub.org). These hubs are typically operated by co-op food stores that use their warehouses as drop-off points for farmers. Within twenty-four hours of delivery, a small staff coordinates the sales of the produce and the distribution of the fresh produce to stores, hospitals, school cafeterias, food banks, institutions, restaurants, and households. The farmer must register his farm with the hub online, itemize all of his or her products with a price list, and list the available produce daily. A store or restaurant can look up what produce is available and order directly from the farmer. Once or twice a week the farmer drops off all the orders, and those who have placed an order can pick up the fresh produce hours after the delivery. It's a slick concept that is gaining ground in small communities, but has some problems. I've been involved with a program for a year and the hub has been a disaster for this small farmer. The problem is that the people who set up these concepts have never been farmers, but were employees of the big distribution systems, and it ends up that the hub becomes just another outlet for the big distributors. Until the farmer comes first this system is just another drop-off for companies like UNFI, Veritable Vegetable, and others. Hubs have to be brokers for small farmers. In large cities like Reno, with over 227,000 people, the Great Basin Community Food Co-op hub should be able to sell everything a dozen or so small farmers can give them. Instead, these employees have never taken the time to even come out to our farms; they sit behind a desk with their iPhone and call distributors three hundred miles away and order the same crap (industrial produce) that goes to all the other stores and is a week old. Meanwhile, us small farmers get an order for a couple of bunches of radishes and a few carrots, which is not worth our effort to drive it in fifty miles to Reno. Unless we as small farmers find more markets, we will struggle to move freshly picked, local produce within our communities. In these hubs, there are no sales people assigned to help farmers sell local produce. They put in their eight hours and go home. Farmers need dedicated middlemen who have small farmers as their main interest and priority that can reach out to the 95 percent of the public that are still using the chain grocery stores. If we don't find a system soon, we are not going to attract any new farmers because they will have nowhere to sell their produce, and it's only a matter of time before we lose the existing ones.

Buying local shouldn't just stop at "buying." We also need to consider the end result, which is "wasting." Communities must take advantage of the recycling movement to manage their green waste by coordinating delivery of all perishable goods to food banks and pantry kitchens for the needy, and to composting sites at the landfills. Americans consume and dispose of more waste than any other country in the world. Plastic, plastic, and more plastic—everything plastic is packaged in plastic. Most small farmers and local crafters sell their goods free of packaging. The produce is a fresh bunch of radishes, not a sealed bag of nicely peeled, bite-sized carrots with reduced nutritional value. In buying local you can avoid adding your footprint to the environment by selecting renewable packaging like wood, glass, metal, cardboard, paper, and biodegradable products. Small farmers practice low-impact farming, whereby we try to improve our soils with minimal tillage, reduce soil compaction by not using heavy equipment, build healthy soil by composting and utilizing "green manure" practices, and do mostly everything manually by hand. Buying from a small farmer reduces fossil fuel use, and is better for the environment, while factory farms use tons of fossil fuels for their big tractors and equipment, commercial fertilizers, pesticides, packaging and marketing products, and advertising labels. The buy-local movement has to be full circle and a community effort.

We all have to work together to bring the spirit of local communities back into society, and it will stimulate our local economies by creating jobs and keeping our money at home. Invest in your future, which means local jobs and businesses for your children.

You know, this past Christmas Eve I watched Jim Carrey's *How the Grinch Stole Christmas* with my fourteen-year-old son, Joey, and I thought to myself, even though this is a funny movie and unrealistic, just think if local communities were that *together*. Despite the Grinch stealing all the presents on Christmas Eve, nobody really cared about material things; it was about the spirit of Christmas, a time for giving what matters most, family, friendship, and humanity. The Grinch's heart grew as he realized the meaning of Christmas, and our hearts have to grow as well, to understand the meaning of buying local. That's the spirit that we need in order to make the buy-local movement work. It's not about easy and convenient but about doing the right thing to save our small farmers and businesses across America. So remember to "put up" and buy local, and help make this ship sail. Or "shut up" and go to Costco. It's your choice, but don't drag the farmer through the mud if you're not going to be serious about it.

Slow Food Versus Fast Food: Lifestyle and Health

The saying "we've come a long way baby" doesn't apply here, because we've actually gone a long way backwards living the unhealthy American lifestyle. Let's face it; a lot of Americans are lazy, unhealthy, and fat. If Nonno was living today, he would have told them in his Italian accent, "Ay, you get off your fat ass, eat good, and go to work! You need some exercise!" Well said, simple as that!

If you look back at history you can pretty much figure out where we went wrong to become a complacent, sedentary, unhealthy, and overweight society. It all began with the loss of the American small farmer and the beginning of industrial farming after World War II. We went from the field to the chair. Up until the 1960s over 10 percent of Americans were active in farming. We ate fresh fruits and vegetables; had plenty of exercise; and the kids rode bikes, swam in creeks, threw rocks, and climbed trees. Industrial farming and later the high-tech industries—television, computers, video games, iPods, and cellular phones—changed our lives. People left the wide-open farm fields, took off their blue-collar shirt to put on a nice white-collar shirt, and went to work miles away, to an office in a high-rise building. As time progressed, women began to pursue their own careers and as the economy got tougher, some needed to work in order to help the family make ends meet. That changed the dynamics of the family life. Nobody was home to get Jimmy off to school, or to cook for him when he got home. Mom and Dad grabbed McDonald's on the way home from work while Jimmy sat on the couch and watched TV or played his video games until somebody came home with dinner. That scenario has changed the American lifestyle and contributed to an unhealthy society. We have lost the family structure—the home life of dads, moms, kids, and grandparents working together, eating and socializing together, and vacationing together. Today everyone goes his or her own way. "I'll catch a bite when I can. See you when I get home." Once Dad gets home, it's plop on the couch to watch sports with a quadruple chalupa, a sixty-ounce soda, and some greasy onion rings. The kids get home and get on their Xbox, iPads, iPods, and text friends on cell phones for hours. Meanwhile, Mom "zaps" something in the microwave, turns on *Desperate Housewives* reruns, and gets on Facebook or Twitter to talk to her girlfriends. Around ten o'clock at night, Dad is passed out on the couch, the kids haven't done their homework, and Mom is still online. Where's the family structure, the healthy food, or the exercise? That's the American household! No wonder obesity and diabetes are at epidemic proportions, and the end of heart disease and cancers are nowhere in sight.

Not only have the industrial and high-tech revolutions been a major factor in the decline of healthy lifestyles, but the revolution of fast food and the emergence of factory foods have joined the bandwagon too. The fast food and corn industry saw that people had no time to cook because they were always on the run, and the TV and electronics industries saw that they were a perfect match—folks could just plop down on the couch with a greasy burger at the end of the day. Truly a match made in heaven! So how do we extinguish the monster we created? How do we get people to eat fruits and vegetables and exercise? Europe figured it out right away when the first McDonald's appeared in Rome. A man named Carlo Petrini quickly started the Slow Food movement in Italy, realizing that the concept of fast food would destroy the enjoyment of sitting down with your family and slowly savoring the food, wine, and conversation. Gee, I wonder if it's working in Europe, this slow food thing? Well, some European countries have the lowest rates of heart disease, diabetes, and heart attacks, and the residents often drink more wine and live longer. We could learn a thing or two from these slow food folks, don't you think? In the United States, we have gotten so far from that, it's all on the go, no time to eat right or to talk. I'll just text you as I'm driving or even walking right next to you. It blows me away to see young people texting someone that is a few feet in front of them. In the future, will we even know how to carry on a conversation? The American society seems to be going in the wrong direction, a direction of superficial materialism, not sustainable, a consume-and-dispose-of society, and just eating the cheapest, most nonnutritious foods available.

Throughout this book, I talk about the obstacles and struggles small farmers go through, and that farming is hard work, but we are the ones producing healthy foods for Americans. Americans know that they should be exercising, and eating fresh fruits and vegetables, but they don't because the Frankenfood (GMO) and fast food giants keep twisting the story, their labels, and their advertisements to convince Americans that they're providing Jimmy with a healthy chalupa. Wake up, America! It's another corn-based product to make you fat! The bottom line is that we have to get off our asses, exercise, and eat fruits and vegetables. So, become a small farmer, like me. You are your own boss, you get a lot of exercise, you're out in the fresh air, you can eat fresh vegetables every day, and you get to sit down and have dinner with your family every night. That's the direction America needs to go back to; it's nothing new. We need more small farmers to bring that 1 percent back to the 40 or 50 percent. There is no "unemployment" on the farm; there is always something to do and grow, and everyone has to eat.

As I stated in Chapter 7, small farmers have to continually diversify their operations to make a living, and I realize that us small farmers have not been capitalizing on one major element that can put us over the top: exercise. Americans get around being lazy by saying, "You know I have an office job, so to get some exercise I'll join a gym and work out before or after work, and that will keep me in shape." Wrong! In reality, they sit on their asses, eat fast food, and graze throughout the day, then go pay a membership to lift a few weights or ride a bike. Hell, why didn't I think of that? I think all small farmers across America should start our own exercise clubs, not in a stuffy, sweaty gym but outside, in the fresh air, on our farms. We'll call it FARMERCISE! Instead of us paying interns or farm workers, the overweight, out-of-shape American public can join our farmercise club and come do our farm work for one or two hours a day. You can work your biceps and your quads by moving irrigation pipes, do your squats by picking vegetables and lifting crates of produce, complete your reps through the monotonous pulling of weeds and picking of tree fruits, and get your cardio by riding your bike to and from your local farm. In addition, you get to take a basket of fruits and vegetables home every day to your family. What a workout! Beats any gym I know. Just think, you are creating a healthy body, changing your lifestyle, knowing and experiencing where your food comes from, and supporting a small family farm. Now who wants to go to a smelly, stinky gym and pedal an exercise bike going nowhere with your nose behind someone's ass on a bike in front of you? Wouldn't you rather farm?

Changing our lifestyle in America is going to be a challenge. We are a runaway train in corporate America. The 1 Percent runs this country, and we are a bunch of lemmings heading aimlessly off the cliff. The only way we can change this unhealthy lifestyle is with baby steps. Try some baby steps at home. If you have to buy fast food, instead of taking home a big greasy burger and fries, give up the fries and add a salad. Take on the concept of everything in moderation. Drink water or juice instead of a sixty-ounce diet soda. Add exercise to your lifestyle, simple things like walking out to check the mail instead of driving or walking to a small restaurant for lunch instead of driving. Take out a section of your backyard lawn and add a garden. You might be surprised by how peaceful it is to garden, and it will help reduce your stress levels in dealing with the hustle and bustle of urban life.

People have to reacquaint themselves with healthy foods, organic fruits and vegetables, and getting plenty of exercise. They have to slow down and make a commitment to themselves, just like they had to do to support the buy-local movement.

Our health in America has declined not only due to changes in our lifestyle and the introduction of factory foods, but also by the influence of the corporate health industry. The pharmaceutical, insurance, and health professional industries have seriously contributed to an unhealthy America. We have the best doctors in the world, but the worst health system of the developed countries. Healthcare costs have gone through the roof over the past years, to the point that it's a major crisis in America. Most families can't afford health care. We are no exception. Kim and I dropped our health insurance in 2010 because we couldn't afford it anymore. We keep Joey's because he's young and plays sports. We had the "catastrophic plan" with Blue Cross, a $5,000 deductible, and it was costing us $700 each quarter. What a joke. I'll just put that money in the bank, eat my fruits and vegetables, get my exercise on the farm, and hope for the best. That's all you can do. The healthcare system is a mess in America. All you see on TV are pharmaceutical ads every two minutes pushing another drug. They're the drug dealers that are killing Americans, and people worry about pot! I say, legalize marijuana; at least it's a natural drug, not a synthetic alien that's going to eat your guts out!

The problem with our health system in America starts with our health professionals. For years, the mentality of our health professionals has been to treat the symptoms, not the cause. "Just take these four tablets a day and the pain will go away." But the pain is still there, because the doctors didn't cure the problem; they just made it go away. It's cause and effect because the drug they give you causes another symptom or a side effect, so they can give you another drug to treat that symptom, a treatment that causes another symptom, and so on. Like the song says, "the beat goes on, and the beat goes on." Our health professionals are the pimps for the pharmaceutical companies, pushing pills to the American public, not trying to make a healthier America. Preventative medicine is no secret; other countries do it. It's all about eating healthy foods, getting plenty of exercise, being happy, and living a low-stress lifestyle. It also helps to have good genes and a little luck in life. We don't practice much preventative medicine in America because it would put all the health professionals, health insurance, and pharmaceutical companies out of business.

To me, everything is simple. Have you noticed that? In order to reduce healthcare costs, we need healthier Americans.

We know that if we eat right, exercise, reduce stress, and be happier, we live longer, productive lives. The best way to do that is to stay out of the doctor's office. Do all of the above and get your blood pressure and cholesterol checked annually, do your mammograms and prostrate checks at the clinics when you are supposed to, and don't watch those pharmaceutical ads on TV. My dad, Lou, is a good example: He's eighty-six years old, was born with a midwife, lived an active, healthy life farming eating fresh fruits and vegetables, still runs around everywhere, and likes a brandy and a few glasses of wine at dinnertime. He's never spent a day of his life in the hospital! The healthcare system would go broke on people like Lou Romano!

Of course I have a solution to the healthcare problem in America, but I really think it's just common sense. I kid about a lot of things in life, and this subject is no different. I think the American health professionals are the best in the world, and that there is a place for our health insurance and pharmaceutical companies, but right now it's all about corporate greed, not about what's best to make a healthier America. To me, that's what's really sad. My solution is a simple one. I feel every person in American should have an even start; how they finish the race is up to them. We should start the race with socialized medicine. Basic, preventative care should be free, and that includes: education on healthy diets, foods, fruits and vegetables; exercise; homeopathic remedies and medicines; holistic practices such as acupuncture, yoga, and massage therapy; chiropractic care; psychiatric and mental health care; and pediatric care. In addition, annual checkups, screenings, and walk-in visits for colds, the flu, scrapes, minor injuries, aches and pains, and allergies should all be free. This socialized preventative medicine plan would be run by small community clinics, housing doctors, nurse practitioners, nurses, and the list of the above preventative medicine professionals. All of this care would be subsidized up to $5,000 per individual, $10,000 per family. Everything else would be considered a "catastrophic" plan, and you could buy whatever plan you wanted from Blue Cross, Blue Shield, or any other insurance company. The incentive here would be for the American public to start out with healthy lives for free, without the burden of expensive healthcare costs that they can't afford. They'd then be rewarded the rest of their lives for continuing to eat right, exercise, and stay healthy. The socialized medicine plan shows that Uncle Sam cares, and that it's an American's right to at least start out having paid health care. We do need an option; we can't be at the mercy of the healthcare system as we are today. There's no way our health system will ever sustain itself on the path that it is currently on. It's an example of why we have economic woes today: greed and selfishness are destroying the American public, and we need to go back to what this country was founded on, which was hard work and working together loyally and honestly to find solutions to our problems. It all starts with a healthy lifestyle of family values, low stress, exercise, and eating fresh, organic fruits and vegetables. If we can at least take these baby steps to make ourselves healthier, we will be a happier, friendlier, sustainable, and more productive America.

Chapter 10
WHY I FARM

Italians come to ruin most generally in three
ways: women, gambling, and farming. My family
chose the slowest one.

~Pope John XXIII

Why do you farm? In today's world, you can ask any
small American farmer this question, and each one will
probably give you a different answer. The one common thread
that keeps us small farmers connected comes from the heart.
It's our desire and passion to farm the land, plain and simple.
Speaking for myself, there were plenty of times that I could
have thrown in the towel and gone back to that secure job with
parks and recreation, but there was always my drive to sustain
the farm. Maybe I was trying to prove to myself that I could be
a successful farmer like my dad, and his father before him. On
the other hand, maybe Kim is right when she says, "You're in
denial," in that we haven't been able to make a decent living,
all the get-rich farming schemes have failed to get us out of the
red, and the only way we've survived is by getting bailed out by
Dad every winter. All I know is that for whatever reason, Sierra
Valley Farms is still here, coming down the home stretch. We
might be leaking oil and puffing smoke, but I can see the finish
line!

No matter what the reason, farming allows you to forget
all the problems at home or in the world. You're at peace with
yourself. It's just you and the earth, and if you take care of
and feed the earth, it will feed you back. There isn't a more
important person on Earth than the farmer. We grow your
food, we are the prime stewards of the land, we create habitats
for animal and plant life, and we build strong local economies

and communities. To be a farmer is the ultimate reward, providing food for life. The earth is your land of opportunity. As Nonno said to us when we were kids, "If you've got land, you can grow anything. If you need more money, you grow more crops. You're your own boss, and nobody tells you what to do!" He was right, and to this day if I need more money I plant, plant, and plant. As for the rewards, there is no better feeling than watching those seedlings come out of the ground, seeing that nicely weeded row of spring mix as you look back at your labors, or using that first big heirloom tomato you pick to make a BLT. But the ultimate reward is watching the glow in your customers' faces when they tell you that the organic vegetables you provide for their family are the best they've ever had. It really doesn't get any better than that! It's what fuels the addiction to farm—that passion, to get back to the earth, and make things grow. (See my YouTube video "Passion for the Land: Is Sustainable Attainable?" produced by the University of California Agriculture and Natural Resources Division.) Like any other passion in life, it comes from within your heart and soul. It's something you were meant to do. I was meant to farm. I fought it as a child, as most kids would do, got as far away as I could from it in my early adulthood, but then returned because it was a part of me that was missing—it was definitely a full metamorphosis. The *egg-larva* stage was my childhood, during which both sides of my family exposed me to farming. Then came the *nymph-pupa* stage in which I resembled an adult but went into hibernation (my career in parks and recreation as my "cocoon") only to emerge as an *adult* farmer. It has been a complete life cycle for this farmer. As I think back over my last fifty years in and out of farming, with all the experiences, good and bad, I feel that I am street smart about surviving as a small farmer in the twenty-first century. What I took for granted— my farming heritage—has now become unique, almost extinct, like a dinosaur (or shall we say a farmasaur?). That's why I want to share my story. I'm not sure many kids today, or in the near future, are going to have a childhood influenced by an old-fashioned farming and ranching family.

No other occupation has been around since the start of civilization. Early dwellers realized that all food comes from the earth, and all plants produce seeds that fall to the earth and create life. The passion to farm and grow Mother Nature's garden started long ago. "You can take the farm away from the farmer, but you can't take farming away from the farmer." It's what drives us, at least the Romano family. Farming is hard work and long hours, and when a crop is ready to be harvested, all vacations and holidays are scrapped because you have to make hay while the sun shines. Unless you're a farmer or rancher, and you do this for a living, not a hobby, it's hard to explain the feeling of starting the season, when you turn the first piece of ground and see all that rich, organic, deep loam, full of worms and organic matter. There is no other smell like fresh turned topsoil, as you run it through your fingers and smell the whole world in your hand. Did you know that there are more than two million different microbes in a handful of healthy, organic soil? Many of them have yet to be identified. Like Marty Feldman said in *Young Frankenstein*, "It's ALIVE. IT'S ALIVE!" and yes, it is. There is nothing on Earth that sustains more life than soil. Small farmers are the architects of the earth, the artists, who use their own imagination, knowledge, and creativity to grow their masterpieces. They create an oasis within the microclimates and parameters of their farms. I saw that through Nonno and my dad and mom; it was just effortless for them to grow anything they wanted, using no fertilizers or pesticides. We never fought insect pests or had puny flowers. The florists would always boast about the Romanos having the best flowers and blossoms in the flower market. Even today, at eighty-six years old, Dad's eyes lights up when spring comes around and it's time to turn the ground over. He'll say, "Hey, do you have anything that I can disk?" I'll say, "Sure, go ahead." And as he's disking with that John Deere tractor—the dust flying, his one hand on the back wheel well and the other on the steering wheel as he looks back at the rows of turned soil, and the cloud of blackbirds following him like he's throwing out bird seed—I know what he's feeling. He is in heaven! I will always remember Dad coming in for dinner after disking or rototilling the fields; he looked like a coal miner, every inch of him covered in dirt. Mom would say, "You better shake all that dirt off outside. Don't bring it in the house!" As he walked back out the door there was a puff of dust with every step, just like Pig-Pen, the *Peanuts* cartoon character. Dad would smile, laugh, and say, "Yes, dear." Even his front teeth were covered in dirt, but I know he wouldn't have wanted it any other way. I didn't realize at the time because I was too young, but now that I think back, he was doing what he loved in life, and that's what I wanted to do when I grew up: be just like Dad.

My brother, Larry, and I would laugh, because throughout all the eminent domains, deaths in the family, farming woes, and declines in the flower business, Dad and Mom could always make a living basically selling weeds, in the middle of Silicon Valley, in the most expensive county (San Mateo) in the country. We figured that if a holocaust ever came, the only thing left on Earth would be the cockroaches, the coyotes, and the Romanos!

Is Farming Suicide with a Butter Knife?

As I look back at this small organic farmer's journey and the "stages" that I have gone through over the years, I'm always trying to evaluate what makes a sustainable farm. One of my goals in writing this book was to explain my life and experiences so that other farmers could look at their own journeys and hopefully avoid my failures and reap the benefits of my successes. In Appendix C, I've added a list, "Ten Ways Farmers Can Sustain the Family Farm in the Twenty-First Century." In today's world there are a lot of factors that have to go right in order to sustain a small family farm, but the main answer is right in the description itself—"family farm." That's why it's called a family farm; it's all about the family running the farm, *la familia*! That's what's missing today in America, the family unit. If the family structure is not there to support farmers and their farms, they will not endure the stresses and obstacles of the farming lifestyle. Today 40 to 50 percent of all marriages fail and there are few occupations that can stress a marriage more than a family farm. As I look back on Grandpa Folchi's ranches and what my Dad and Nonno had in the flower business, the common denominator was the family unit, all working together like spokes in a wheel to make a living on the land. Running Sierra Valley Farms, I've been able to jump through all of the hoops and around all the obstacles to get certified organic, or to get financing, or to diversify my crops, products, and markets to make a living, but the one component that I don't have is the "family buy-in" that my parents and grandparents had in past years. Times are different, and even though you raise your family on a farm, the influences of the twenty-first century are everywhere. The lures of media, society, and technology make a deep impression on the family core, even living in rural Plumas County, in Beckwourth, California, with a population of four hundred. Even though we live out in the country, we still fight with our kids to get off the video games, the Xbox, the iPod. Joey has everything that the kids have in the big cities: the clothes, the style, the "talk," and all the high-tech gadgets. It's really difficult to try to teach small farm values and work ethics to a fourteen-year-old when at school all the "real world" values of society are imposed on them: fast food, texting for hours, video games for hours, sleeping in until noon, and that work is a four-letter word. The other part of the puzzle is your partner, or spouse. Growing up in a tight Italian family, everybody, the kids, cousins, grandparents, Mom, and Dad, helped. I took things for granted because Mom was by Dad's side all the time. I'm sure she carried every bunch of flowers that Dad ever cut. As a matter of fact, she didn't even drive; they went everywhere together—shopping, socializing, dancing—and worked together on the farm. The only place she didn't go was to the flower market early in the morning, mainly because she was getting us kids off to school and doing chores around the house. In most small farms, labor is what kills you. You can't afford to hire help, so you try to do it yourself to minimize costs. For a small farmer to have a tight family unit that contributes to the farm is huge. It will make or break you. That is our case here at Sierra Valley Farms: as the years have passed I find myself being somewhat of a one-man army, and it's hard to convince the family that there is a future in farming. It's hard work for little monetary reward. Unless your passion is to farm most other people don't see the value in it. The concept of "this is your dream, not mine" has resonated throughout our family for years, and maybe I should have taken a closer look at the lifestyle that I dragged everybody into. At this farm, we don't have the family unit that is going to take us through the mud of the twenty-first century. I find myself in my mid-fifties doing all the planning, billing, planting, and marketing, and most of the harvesting. I'm getting tired, and as much as I love farming, it would be nice to have some inspiration and support. It's a whole different world to those who don't have the passion to farm. It's hard to sustain the farm by yourself *and* support a family. Every small farmer's fear is to lose the family farm; that each crop may be the last crop he or she will ever sell. The slow death of losing a family farm is suicide with a butter knife for a farmer. Most farmers can see that the end is coming way before it actually happens. Nothing seems to work for them: crops, markets, and financing all fail, and in the end, family and personal self-esteem crumble to the point that all is lost. You just don't walk away and rent a new farm; you have lost yourself, the artist in you, and your life's work. It's a major life change to get a job working for somebody, or moving into a small house in the city. The once-free lion is now a caged animal in the city or suburbs, and has to adapt to neighbors. It's something I don't think I could ever do again. Over the last twenty years of squeaking by, I know my farm has a slow leak and is limping down the road. I'm not getting any younger; I don't see my family getting more involved, and it's going to be a long time before we see any major changes in America to help the small family farmer. It's like I'm winning some of the battles, but losing the war. But you just do the best you can while you're here on Earth, and be happy that this is the life you chose. I truly believe timing is everything in life, and if a small farmer can hang on long enough, he or she will be able to sustain the farm. If you are fortunate enough to sustain the farm, sacrifices have likely been made because the longevity of a small farm is always in question, and few survive. For this farmer, if farming is suicide with a butter knife, I can't think of a better way to go!

Looking to the Future

Over the years, I've avoided adding a livestock element to the farm because I physically could not take on another venture, and the family had no interest in farm animals. The last three years I have been blessed to have an apprentice, Ryan Keisling; I became his mentor and have been teaching him the farming techniques of the Sierra. He has become a vital part of Sierra Valley Farms, and has a passion to raise organic and biodynamic livestock and create artisan cheeses here in Sierra Valley. He recently invested into Sierra Valley Farms, and was considering adding a livestock element. Being an ex-executive chef, with culinary work in Italy, New York, Boston, and Lake Tahoe, Ryan has taught this dirt farmer how to grow the specialty crops that chefs want and about the value of organic free-range poultry, pork, lamb, rabbit, raw milk, and artisan cheeses. We're quite a team. Both somewhat extreme in our thinking—kind of out there probably to most—neither of us care about the money; we just want to make ends meet and have a nice life. We do it for the lifestyle and because it's the right thing to do—grow and provide organic, sustainable, healthy foods for you.

We have discussed taking fifty-five acres of fallow pastures and turning them into a mosaic of moveable heritage chicken and turkey tractors and paddocks (chicken houses on wheels), four lean-to corrals with ten to fifteen adjoining acres where we would rotate a half dozen hogs, twenty to thirty sheep, twenty to thirty turkeys, and a milk cow and a milking goat or two, and maybe a small rabbit hutch. We may start small with egg production and a few animals. This is all based on proven sustainable models that the granddad of them all, Virginia farmer Joel Salatin, has set up in his farming operations and made so famous. The trick would be to modify them to adapt to the harsher climate here in Sierra Valley. Ideally, we'll grow our own feed and thresh our own grain for the animals then turn them onto our six acres of vegetables in the fall, after harvest, to crap their brains out on our vegetable crops, and then turn the crops under for the winter.

Ryan and I met with my Uncle Emilio, now ninety-two years old, in December 2012; I bought the farm from him in 1989. We wanted to ask him about how they ran the livestock operations in his heyday and as we explained that we were thinking about it, he first laughed, and then said, "You guys are crazy. What do you want to do that for?" As we explained the potential small scale operation and our rotation, Emilio quickly came on board and was a wealth of knowledge, sharp as a tack, still remembering the exact varieties of rye, winter wheat, hard or soft wheat, and pasture grasses. He also recommended the breeds of hogs, chickens, cows, lambs, sheep, and goats and how to tend to them in the harsh climate of Sierra Valley, giving us plenty of his tricks of the trade. The knowledge of these old-timers will be gone some day, and Ryan and I listened very attentively to what he had to say. What's great about vintage farmers and ranchers is that they always go off on a tangent and tell stories over and above the original subject. As Emilio got more comfortable, he popped open a bottle of homemade apricot grappa and poured Ryan and me a healthy shot; he then kicked it into high gear and talked about how they lost the dairy industry in 1950 when the railroads cut out the service delivery to Oakland and San Francisco and went only with freight. The farmers in Sierra Valley could not move any more milk to the big dairies in the Bay Area, and they soon died out. In addition to the loss of the dairies, there was no need for farmers to produce grain, so pasture for beef cattle became a priority. At about that time, in the 1960s, chemical companies solicited farmers to crop dust their acres of sagebrush with Agent Orange to kill the sagebrush and then reseed pasture land for beef cattle instead of dairy cows. In the process, farmers had to flag the planes as to where the pilots were to release the chemicals over their fields. With no protective gear, the farmers were covered with gallons of these toxic pesticides. Emilio went on to say that he only did it once because he knew it was wrong. He was right: that spring the pregnant cows that were sprayed had deformed births, and aborted about 30 percent of their young. To complicate this, Emilio said that many of the farmers thought the spraying was great and sprayed as much as they could, and within twenty to thirty years most of those ranchers died from cancer. Emilio had so many stories to tell, we could have stayed for hours. It was so important for Ryan and me to ask as many questions as possible in order to duplicate how my uncles and grandparents farmed and ranched in Sierra Valley in the old days, and how they sustained the ranches from 1907 to 1975. Ryan and I left with an understanding of "the old ways," and with more confidence about adding a livestock operation, if we decided to go in that direction.

On our drive home we both realized that the way Emilio explained how they did things in the old days was that "it wasn't a big deal," you just did it. It was very simple, not complicated—just common sense and having a base knowledge of how ecosystems work and the biodynamic process that take place.

I am excited about this venture because it could complete the farm. To achieve full efficiency of our land and to sustain our operation and the ecological balance of our nutrient cycle, allowing plant and animal biprocesses to enhance our fertility program, is a goal.

Writing this book and another next year is another venture that hopefully will help support Sierra Valley Farms, and help fund our "going green" mission to reduce costs and our environmental footprint, to install solar, and to transform our equipment to biodiesel. In addition, my mission at this point in my life is to inspire new farmers, young and old, to assist us old-timers in going back to the old ways of life, creating a wholesome environment for our families, and providing fresh, organic food for our communities.

Either way, you just ride that wave through life until it dumps you out at the end. Life's good! I don't see myself ever selling the farm; I'm going down with ship. *Why I Farm* best describes the metamorphosis that I have gone through because, in the end, the small family farmer figures it out one way or the other, but not without consequences, which sometimes means losing his or her family, the farm, or both, or having to sell out and walk away from a farmer's identity and lifestyle. As I was writing this book I thought to my self, "Why do I farm?" I've worked a lot of jobs in my life from sales to a garbage man, a park ranger, and a cushy park superintendent job in Lake Tahoe. I must say that in the end I was born to farm. It has to be the most rewarding job I've ever done. But it's not a job to me; it doesn't feel like work, it feels like a way of life. It's about having a passion; it's about being free, just you and the elements that Mother Nature provides. The farm is an open picture frame that you make a mosaic art form; it's your creation, your masterpiece. I farm because there isn't a more important person in this world than a farmer that provides food for his or her fellow humans. Thousands of years ago, our society was one of hunters and gatherers, and when those gatherers began using crude tools to dig up bulbs and plant seeds they became farmers. It was and still is a way of life. It's not work; work is a four-letter word that was created for something you don't like to do. Farming is a lifestyle, and that lifestyle involves independence, self-sufficiency, being your own boss, and being able to create as much or as little income as you see fit. The economy really doesn't play a role in your success as a farmer because everyone has to eat—the key to success is finding your niche in the food society, and being progressive and innovative to sustain your farm. You just can't put all your eggs in one basket; you must constantly diversify your operation and stay driven and motivated for the cause. It's a lot of hard work and dedication, but it's not just about a monetary reward.

The reward is in the quality of life, and this is why I farm.

Appendix A
THE CORNER STORE FARMERS' MARKET:
A MODEL FOR SMALL, RURAL COMMUNITIES

Introduction

Using San Francisco as an example, there are very few major supermarkets in the city, even today. Yes, land is a limiting factor, but parking space is at a premium so most residents depend on their local corner grocery store for the majority of their groceries like dairy products, juices, canned goods, meats, liquors, and produce. Traveling in and out of San Francisco is a major obstacle, so for many people the benefit of convenience is well worth the added price they pay at the corner grocery store. The corner store concept can play a major role in establishing farmers' markets in rural and suburban communities.

History and Trends in Farmers' Markets

Over the past ten years, farmers' markets have emerged at an astounding rate nationwide. California still leads the nation in farmers' markets, and has set the standards for other states to follow. Being a certified agricultural producer for the last thirteen years and attending more than eighty farmers' markets a year from Marin County, California, to Reno, Nevada, I've watched farmers' markets grow by leaps and bounds. The way they've been established over the last ten years involves a community with a need and usually taps into an existing farmers' market network that a nonprofit association or a public entity has set up regionally; they then apply to CDFA to certify the market with the State of California and submit bylaws. Once approved, the entity then finds a centralized location for the market, hires a manager, recruits as many farmers and crafters as it can, establishes a capacity level, and charges a stall fee. All farmers, food vendors, and crafters must be grouped together, and they now promote the market to the community. The farmers must be certified agricultural producers through the County Agricultural Commissioners office, verifying that the crops listed are the ones grown on their farms. You may sell for two other farmers only, and they and their crops must be listed. These forms must be posted at your stall at the farmers' market, and all vendors today are required to carry at least a two-million-dollar liability insurance to attend a market. The stall fees range from thirty to fifty dollars for a ten-by-ten-foot stall. Usually there are annual fees for these farmers' market associations.

Over the last five years, farmers' markets have become so popular that growers are hustling to get into them to sell their products. Farmers' markets and CSAs are about the only way small farmers can get their product to the consumer in any volume. The large food chains are tied to distributors, and there are a few co-op stores that will deal with farmers directly. Restaurants are for the overflow and are hit-and-miss; it all depends on the chef and the restaurant's dedication to buying local.

What's happened in the last few years is that communities, farmers' market associations, and managers have installed farmers' markets to bring people to downtown areas, create social events, and make money, thinking the more vendors, the more money they will make on stall fees. They don't consider the farmer, food vendor, or crafter; it's usually all about a good presentation and generating revenues. As a result, the associations and managers are ruining the markets. It's a double-edged sword—you need vendors so that people come, and you need a certain volume of people to support the farmers and vendors. But at the markets that I attend, there are way too many of the same type of farmers and vendors than there are volumes of people to support them. Competition is good, but if your farmers' markets are only attracting a few hundred people and you have five tomato and peach growers competing for that one customer, the prices and volume of sales drop drastically. Farmers' markets are actually now hurting certain farmers, and I know of farmers who have dropped 50 percent of their sales because there are too many farmers selling the same product and not enough people buying from each vendor. I know it's a supply-and-demand issue, to a certain point. Farmers' markets have to balance between grower competition and what the market will bear.

The Corner Store Farmers' Market in Operation

Here at Sierra Valley Farms, located in Beckwourth, Plumas County, California, we established the first on-farm farmers' market in the State of California in 2007. Beckwourth is a community of only four hundred people, and within Plumas County there are only about twenty thousand residences. Our goal was to provide fresh produce for our community.

Before 2007, we had a produce stand on the farm for ten years. We could not keep up with the volume of produce needed, so we decided to establish a farmers' market. With over three hundred dedicated weekly customers over the years, we felt it was time to bring in more growers.

Our mission was to develop a farmers' market that was in the best interest of the farmers, to promote local farmers, and to be a one-stop shop for our customers. We set out to select only one or two vendors in the following categories that could provide the best quality with the most diversity: organic vegetables, fruits and berries, wild and fresh fish, local meat (beef, lamb, and pork), wine and cheese, pasta, baked goods and pastries, oils and vinegars, sauces, condiments, jams and jellies, and nuts and grains. We also added a craft vendor and guest chef cooking demonstrations as an attraction. We wanted minimum competition among vendors so they all made a lot of money for traveling such a long distance.

Success

Our on-farm farmers' market has become a huge success for Sierra Valley Farms, the farmers, and the patrons. Our farmers' market begins the first week in June and continues every Friday from 10 a.m. to 2:30 p.m. for sixteen weeks. It has become a destination farmers' market—people are traveling from an hour away to experience the on-farm atmosphere, enjoy the free chef cooking demonstrations, and mingle with our vendors while enjoying samples and wine tasting. Attendance has reached over four hundred people every Friday, and the farmers are generating a much greater income at our farmers' market than they are at the larger farmers' markets in Reno and the Bay Area. Our growers have unanimously rated our farmers' market as the best they have attended, based on customer service, volume of income, and having the friendliest and most loyal customer base. It is a model that is working.

The Corner Store Farmers' Market Model

Mission statement: To provide a farmers' market that supports farmers and develops a loyal customer base to sustain the market by emphasizing customer service, a diverse selection of farmers with the highest quality produce, minimal competition and duplication of products, and the opportunity for the local community to access to fresh, local produce and other agricultural products.

Legal Obligations
- Apply to CDFA as a certified farmers' market.
- Obtain appropriate county or city permits.
- Obtain appropriate liability insurance coverage.
- Obtain appropriate environmental health permits.

Community Support
- Select a community that will support a small group of farmers, such as homeowners associations, small towns, CC&R groups, gated communities, and neighborhood community groups.
- Select a location that is a popular spot to congregate, can handle six to twelve vendors, and has adequate parking

and accessibility, such as a local farm, school, park, church, vacant lot, strip mall parking lot, or vacant store.

Farmers' Market

- Create a market that is friendly, attractive, and has a lot to offer. The manager must be customer-service oriented, on-site, and outgoing within the community.

- Select six to twelve farmers/vendors that have the best personality, quality of product, and diversity. Try to carry the basics: organic fruits, nuts and berries, vegetables, local meats, poultry, eggs, fish, a variety of value-added local products, baked goods, and dairy products. Try to also have a couple of the best local food vendors attend.

- Select days and hours that are the most convenient for your community. Weekends work best at midday, but farmers attend a lot of big markets every weekend and are thus hard to secure. Select midweek days between 2 p.m. and 6 p.m. so that people can stop by after work and school to shop.

- Try to feature a special attraction for your market related to food, like chef cooking demonstrations, cookbooks and recipes, book signings, or community talks, or feature a local art fair once a month.

- Minimize duplication of farmers selling the same product so that the farmer you select is making good money to be there. Use the criteria that if you are running out of a product, say tomatoes by mid-market, you can bring in another grower to help meet the demand. Also, if you have a conventional grower selling tomatoes, it's okay to bring in an organic tomato grower to meet customer demands for a variety of quality products.

- Stall price: Try to keep your stall prices for the vendors very reasonable, between twenty and thirty dollars, and be flexible. If they have had a slow day, reduce your price for that day.

Benefits of a Corner Store Farmers' Market

- Increases access for farmers to sell more products
- Increases availability of local, fresh produce to a wide variety of communities
- Provides fresh produce to people in communities that would not ordinarily attend large farmers' markets miles away
- Creates a "neighborhood," or social atmosphere for the community
- Creates a know-your-farmer, know-where-your-food-comes-from personal relationship with your farmer
- Is convenient for people in your community, providing them with easier access to fresh produce without having to travel miles away
- Is an educational tool for your local community
- Provides additional income for the landowner of the market site

Appendix B
RESOURCES FOR SMALL FARMERS

Organic Certification
California Certified Organic Farmers (CCOF)
    www.ccof.org
California Certified Producers Application
    www.cfm@cdfa.ca.gov
Quality Assurance International (QAI)
    www.qai.inc.com
Oregon Tilth
    www.tilth.org
Organic Trade Association (OTA)
    www.ota.com

Farm Directories
Local Harvest
    www.localharvest.com
The New Farm
    www.newfarm.org
California Certified Farmers' Markets
    www.cdfa.ca.gov

Watchdog Groups
Slow Food
    www.slowfood.com
The Sustainable Economies Law Center
    www.theselc.org
Food and Water Watch
    www.foodandwaterwatch.org

Farming Resources
ATTRA National Sustainable Agriculture Information Service
    www.attra.ncat.org

Ecofarm
    www.eco-farm.org
Soil and Plant Laboratory
    www.soilandplantlaboratory.com
High Tunnels
    www.hightunnels.org
Farm Tek
    www.farmtek.com
Commercial Hydroponic Supply
    www.cropking.com
Microsprinklers and Irrigation
    www.dripworksusa.com
Peaceful Valley Farm Supply
    www.groworganic.com
McConkey Horticultural Supply
    www.mcconkeyco.com
Natural Resources Conservation Service (NRCS)
    www.nrcs.usda.gov
United States Department of Agriculture (USDA)
    www.usda.gov
California Department of Food and Agriculture (CDFA)
    www.cdfa.gov
Food and Drug Administration (FDA)
    www.fda.gov
National Young Farmers' Coalition
    www.youngfarmers.org
Worldwide Opportunities on Organic Farms (WWOOF)
    www.wwoof.org

Seed and Plant Catalogs

Johnny's Seeds
    www.johnnyseeds.com
High Mowing Seed Company
    www.highmowingseeds.com

Gourmet Seed International
        www.gourmetseed.com
Italian Seed and Tool Company
        www.italianseedandtool.com
Seed Savers
        www.seedsavers.org
Territorial Seed Company
        www.territorialseed.com
Nourse Berry and Perennial Vegetable Plants
        www.noursefarms.com
Weeks Berry Nursery
        www.weeksberry.com
Seeds of Change
        www.seedsofchange.com
Indiana Berry
        www.indianaberry.com
Wild Garden Seed
        www.wildgardenseed.com
Baker Creek Heirloom Seeds
        www.rareseeds.com
Ronniger Potato Farm
        www.ronnigers.com

Recommended Readings

Abbey, Edward. *The Monkey Wrench Gang.* Salt Lake City: Dream Garden Press, 1985.

Bradbury, Zoë Ida, Severine von Fleming, and Paula Manalo, eds. *Greenhorns.* North Adams: Storey Publishing, 2012.

Goodall, Jane. *Harvest for Hope: A Guide to Mindful Eating.* New York: Warner Books, 2005.

Imhoff, Daniel. *Food Fight: The Citizen's Guide to the Next Food and Farm Bill.* Healdsburg: Watershed Media, 2012.

Katz, Sandor Ellix. *The Revolution Will Not Be Microwaved: Inside America's Underground Food Movements.* White River Junction: Chelsea Green Publishing, 2006.

Kingsolver, Barbara. *Animal, Vegetable, Miracle: A Year of Food Life.* New York: HarperCollins Publishers, 2007.

Pollan, Michael. *In Defense of Food: An Eater's Manifesto.* New York: The Penguin Press, 2008.

———. *The Omnivore's Dilemma: A Natural History of Four Meals.* New York: The Penguin Press. 2006.

Salatin, Joel. *The Sheer Ecstasy of Being a Lunatic Farmer.* Swoope, Virginia: Polyface, 2010.

Timmermeister, Kurt. *Growing a Farmer: How I Learned to Live Off the Land.* New York: W. W. Norton & Company, Inc., 2011.

Appendix C
TEN WAYS FARMERS CAN SUSTAIN THE FAMILY FARM IN THE TWENTY-FIRST CENTURY

1. Find Your Niche
In this competitive and ever-changing world in which we live in you must find a niche that differentiates you from all the rest—something unique and special about your farm, product, or you as a farmer.

2. Don't Put All Your Eggs in One Basket
Just because you've been doing it the same old way all these years doesn't mean it will always stay the same. Be flexible, and have a back-up or contingency plan. Diversify your operation and crops so that if one has a bad year another can pick up the slack. Be creative and continue to research ways to become more efficient or to improve your operation. Don't settle for the status quo.

3. Be Frugal and Seize Opportunities
When you start out don't overextend yourself by buying everything new. It took me twenty years to buy my first new tractor, and the only reason I bought it was because it came with a beer holder! Now, with Craigslist and online used farm equipment websites, you can find almost everything. Farmers are going out of business every day, so look for auctions, barter with locals, trade equipment, and set up borrowing plans with your neighbors. Most equipment sits most of the time: coordinate when you need it with other farmers. Lease land instead of buying, until you find that dream piece of property or farm. Stockpile money so that you have it available when that foreclosure sale happens down the road or that piece of equipment is up for sale at an auction and you can buy it. Take good care of all your equipment and reuse and save all kinds of hardware, parts, and supplies. Nonno would send Larry

and me to construction sites after hours to collect all the nails that had fallen on the ground. We even had to straighten the crooked ones on the anvil. When we went to the dump we came home with more than we brought. One man's junk is another man's treasure.

4. Make It a Family Affair

I can't stress this enough. The family has to have a "buy-in" on the farm, or you cannot sustain the farm. Keep your spouse and kids, parents, cousins, uncles, whoever, involved. Give them a part that they can call their own, but don't burn them out. Labor is the most expensive part of a farm. The more family help you get, the more successful your farm will be.

5. Kill Them with Kindness

I don't know how many times I've seen farmers grumpy. Be happy; kill your customers with kindness. So what if you have to give that customer a free peach or basket of strawberries, it pays back tenfold. It's said that one positive experience travels to four people while a bad one can spread to one hundred. It's all about customer service. Sell yourself, your farm, and your product in a friendly, positive manner, and recruit your employees that way.

6. Develop Good Work Ethics and Be Consistent

Don't be lazy and hire other people to do the dirty and hard jobs. Do it yourself. Carry the concept of "I wouldn't have anyone do the work that I wouldn't do myself." Get into the trenches with your employees when the going gets tough. They will respect you more. Hard work is a good thing. Be consistent with your customers and employees, so they know what to expect. Don't be wishy-washy, or flaky; if you're a hard-ass always be a hard-ass, so they know what to expect. Never assume that your family members or employees know exactly how you like it, they are not mind readers. Take the time to properly show them how you want it done and give them the proper tools to do it.

7. Be a Rock Star and Toot Your Own Horn

Too many farmers don't draw enough attention to themselves, their farm, or the product they produce. Get out there and be visible. Be active in your agricultural community and become well known, and be available to mentor young people, speak at schools, and open up your farm to the public to bring awareness that small farms and farmers are a vital part of America. Toot your own horn for a change, and be that rock star!

8. Be a Jack-of-All-Trades

Don't go into farming blindly. Learn as much as you can along the way. You will use all the trades in farming, not only trades that deal with agricultural crop production and horticulture but plumbing, construction, welding and fabrication, electrical, and mechanical work. Something always has to be built or has to be fixed; it's like life and death and taxes. It will kill your operations budget if you have to hire outside people to build or fix things on the farm. The more you or your family can do on the farm the more sustainable your farm will be.

9. Know Your Legislators

In order to save the family farm, changes must occur at the policy level. Farmers need to have their lawmakers at the city, county, state, and federal level on speed dial. We have to get involved if we are going to make any kind of meaningful change to our way of life and the future of our food supply. Pick up the phone! Write a letter! Attend a meeting! Let your voice be heard.

10. Follow Your Heart and Your Vision

Don't take no for an answer and be persistent. People will try to give you all kinds of advice and tell you that it won't work. Follow your passion, be a visionary, and be true to your heart. If you believe it, make it happen—no ifs, ands, or buts! Living the farming lifestyle is one of the most stressful livelihoods that there is. Make sure you take care of yourself! It's good to get away and recharge the batteries every once in a while. Always take time for number one; you will be happier to be around, and you will make better choices for sustaining the farm.

Gary Romano, owner of Sierra Valley Farms,
photo courtesy of Roger Freeburg

GLOSSARY

acre 43,560 square feet.

agritourism Any agriculturally based operation or activity that brings visitors to the farm.

alluvial soils A fine-grained fertile soil deposited by water slowly flowing over flood plains, lakebeds, or riverbeds.

ammonium nitrate A colorless, crystalline salt manufactured to be used as a nitrogen fertilizer. It is highly leachable, causing nitrate pollution in drinking water.

ammonium sulfate A brownish-gray crystalline salt manufactured to be used as a nitrogen fertilizer containing sulfur. It is highly leachable, causing nitrate pollution in drinking water.

annual A plant that lives its life cycle in one year; germinates, grows, flowers, sets seed, and dies.

aquifer A body of permeable rock, underground, that contains or transmits groundwater.

biodiesel A vegetable or animal fat-based oil used as an alternative diesel fuel for vehicles.

biodiversity The variety of plants and animals in the world or in a particular habitat or ecosystem.

cleat tractor An antique tractor that has steel tracks that provide low impacts to the soil and the ground, bearing pressure allows easy movement.

cover crop A crop grown to suppress weeds, help build organic matter in the soils, improve fertility, and prevent winter soil erosion.

cow-calf operations A management unit that maintains breeding a herd and produces weaned calves. This operation uses cows and bulls as breeding stock to produce calves, and the calves are then usually sold.

disk A farm implement that has rows of concave circular steel disks that turn the soil. Used primarily to incorporate nutrients and turn under weeds into the soil.

ecotourism Involves traveling to areas of natural or ecological interest for an activity or event that brings attention to that environment and improves the well-being of the local people. endogenous: Having an internal cause or origin. Growing within a specific region or microclimate unique to a region.

GMO crops Genetically modified organisms; a plant whose genetic characteristics have been altered using techniques of genetic engineering. In this case, a plant becomes immune to a particular pesticide that can be sprayed over the top to kill weeds.

granary A storehouse for threshed grain.

green manure A nutrient cycle by which turning under green parts of plants into the soil creates a natural compost, adding fertility and organic matter to enrich the soil.

heirloom seeds Seeds that are usually from plants that have been producing a specific varietal seed for generations. Most heirloom varieties are open-pollinated and their seed produces similar characteristics and adaptations as previous generations.

homesteading An act of claiming public land for farming and improving it, to gain outright possession of it after a certain period of time.

madrone A California native evergreen tree that has an attractive, smooth brown bark and displays beautiful red berries in the fall.

manzanita A California native evergreen shrub that has beautiful, smooth brown bark and fragrant white or pink flowers; valued in the cut-flower industry.

microclimate The climate of a small, specific place within a region or ecosystem.

microgreens Specialty lettuces or greens mixes that are harvested as seedlings, "baby" greens that have intense flavors in their infant stages.

monocropping An agricultural practice of growing the same crop year after year on the same piece of land without crop rotation. Known to deplete the soil of fertility.

organic An agricultural production system that sustains the health of soils, ecosystems, and people. It relies on the ecological processes, biodiversity, and cycles adapted to the local conditions, rather than the inputs of man-made synthetic products (from the International Federation of Organic Agriculture Movements)

outhouse An outbuilding containing a pit toilet with no plumbing. The inside has a large flat plank with one or two holes, each with a toilet seat, bridged over an open pit in the ground.

pelts The skin of an animal with the fur on it that is sold for tanning, or to make clothing.

perennial A plant that lives for more than two years. They tend to be either evergreen or deciduous (lose their leaves), and die back in the fall and winter.

pesticide residue levels The pesticide that remains on or in food after they are applied to food crops. The levels of these residues on or in foods often include chemicals that could build up to harmful levels in the body as well as the environment.

plow A farm implement with one or more curved blades that is drawn by a horse or tractor, used for turning over sod or agricultural soils.

rototill A farming tractor or implement used to till the soil. It has a series of curved blades that rotate at high speed, used to prepare soil for a seedbed.

sovereignty In relation to food, the right of the local people to define their own food systems and agricultural practices.

sweetbreads The thymus gland (part of the throat and neck) of a young calf or lamb that is used for food.

subsidy An annual sum of money granted by a government agency to a corporate farmer to plant or not plant a commodity crop such as rice, cotton, soybean, corn, or wheat.

sugar pine A native California conifer tree known to have the largest pinecone of all the pines.

three-on-the-tree A term used to describe the three-speed transmission on vehicle models between 1939 and the mid-

1970s, in which the gearshift lever was located on the steering column.

trusses A framework, typically consisting of rafters, posts, and struts, that supports a roof structure.

value-added product For farms, it is the additional value obtained from a crop after harvest, for example, processing fruits or vegetables to make jams, jellies, pickles, or other condiments.

wasabi A cousin to the horseradish plant that is used in the Japanese culinary world.

Thomson-Shore, our printer, is a member of the Green Press Initiative (GPI) dedicated to environmentally sound publishing. This book is printed on 30 percent postconsumer recycled paper, processed chlorine-free.